CHARLES REILLY & THE LIVERPOOL SCHOOL OF ARCHITECTURE 1904 - 1933

Catalogue of an exhibition
at the Walker Art Gallery, Liverpool,
25 October 1996 – 2 February 1997

JOSEPH SHARPLES

ALAN POWERS   MICHAEL SHIPPOBOTTOM

LIVERPOOL UNIVERSITY PRESS

First published 1996 by
Liverpool University Press
Senate House
Abercromby Square
Liverpool
L69 3BX
and
National Museums & Galleries on Merseyside
William Brown Street
Liverpool
L3 8EL

British Library Cataloguing in Publication Data
A British Library CIP record is available
ISBN 0–85323–901–0

Front cover: (Cat. 148) Edward Chambré Hardman,
Portrait photograph of Charles Reilly, 1924 (The Board
of Trustees of the National Museums & Galleries on
Merseyside: Walker Art Gallery)

Set in 11/13pt Linotron Bembo by
Wilmaset Ltd, Birkenhead, Wirral
Printed and bound in the European Union by
The Alden Press in the City of Oxford

Contents

Foreword

In 1995, what is now the School of Architecture and Building Engineering at the University of Liverpool celebrated its centenary. In its early years under Professor F. M. Simpson it was an important centre of the Arts and Crafts movement, and its work of this period was the subject of the 'Art Sheds' exhibition held at the Walker Art Gallery in 1981. Now we are turning our attention to the years 1904–33 and to Simpson's dynamic successor, Professor Charles Reilly.

Reilly is a major figure in the history of 20th-century architecture in Britain. He was largely responsible for the triumph of University training over the old system of apprenticeship, and he was a powerful advocate of American-style classicism and, later, European modernism. Today, when both the classical and modern traditions are the subject of reassessment, Reilly's achievements and influence deserve our attention. This exhibition looks at Reilly's teaching, the work of some of his outstanding students, and the buildings he designed himself. The selection of exhibits is national and international in scope, reflecting the breadth of influence of Reilly's School, but there is an emphasis on Liverpool and Merseyside. Liverpool's Victorian architecture is famous, but the city also has many important buildings of the early twentieth century which directly or indirectly reflect the influence of Reilly, and this exhibition highlights some of them.

All exhibitions depend on outside help, but in this case we are more widely indebted than usual. We are grateful to all our lenders, acknowledged individually in the catalogue entries, many of whom have not only allowed us to borrow items for display but have supplied information which would otherwise have been unobtainable; to Alan Powers and Michael Shippobottom for their contributions to this catalogue; to the staff of the University of Liverpool School of Architecture and Building Engineering, Liverpool University Archives, the Liverpool University Press, the Liverpool Record Office and Central Library, the Library and Drawings Collection of the Royal Institute of British Architects, and the British School at Rome; and to the very many people who have given valuable help by answering requests for information, and who are acknowledged below.

The exhibition has been researched and co-ordinated by Joseph Sharples, Assistant Curator in the Department of Fine Art. We thank him and the other staff of the National Museums & Galleries on Merseyside who have contributed to the realisation of this project.

Initial research to determine the feasibility of this exhibition was made possible by an award under the Arts Council's Architecture Grants Scheme. We are grateful for this, and to the University of Liverpool and the P. H. Holt Trust for their contributions towards the cost of the exhibition.

Richard Foster
Director
National Museums & Galleries on Merseyside

Julian Treuherz
Keeper of Art Galleries
National Museums & Galleries on Merseyside

Acknowledgements

Bruce Aitken, Adrian Allan, John Allan, Mrs G. M. Allen, Professor J. S. Allen, Bruce Allsopp, Alan Andrews, Paul Arthur, Brian Ashton, Kate Atkinson, Professor M. Awad, Dr Marilyn Baker, Miss G. Bakewell, Einar Bakstad, John Banton, Martin Barnes, Philip Bell, Mary Bennett, Joanne Bibby, Robin Bloxsidge, Dr Quentin Bone, Sylvester Bone, Dr J. M. L. Booker, Mosette Broderick, Michael Brook, Mr and Mrs Peter Browning, Ann P. Bruch, Julian Budden, Linda Burchall, Janice Carpenter, Rev. Peter Cavanagh, Rita Cheung, Clive M. Chipkin, Barbara S. Christen, R. Colwyn Foulkes, Ann Compton, Douglass Cowin, Ruth Cowin, Sylvia Crabtree, David Crellin, Eva Crider, Mark Crinson, Chris Crouch, Kitty Cruft, Austin Davies, Philip Davies, Andrew S. Dolkart, Dr J. W. Docking, John Dougill, Alison Dove, the late Dame Jane Drew, Michael Findlay, Rev. Oliver Forshaw, Michael and Jenny Fuller, Sara Gavin, the late Professor R. Gardner-Medwyn, Eleanor Gawne, Peggy Gearey, Anne Gleave, Janet Gnosspelius, Norman Goodacre, Peter Hagarty, Dr Omar El-Hakim, John Hardie, Dr Roger Harper, Robert Heal, Kay Hoare, Richard Hodges, John Haymes Hogg, Peter Holden, Robin Holliday, Jack Hubbard, Richard Hubbard, Quentin Hughes, Mrs C. W. Hutton, Eric Hyde, Jill Ivy, Mr K. Jaisim, Dr Nigel Jenkins, Mickey King, Andrew Kirk, Sheila Lemoine, John Lightfoot, Jane Lindsay, Luke McKernan, Olwen McLaughlin, Dr M. Makiya, Enid Marx, Glenise Matheson, Thomas Michie, Mrs C. A. and Mr J. Minoprio, Ranmadi Mirchandani, Anthony Mould, Peter Murray, Roger Norris, Anne O'Connor, Mr A. E. B. Owen, Wallace Paice, Alexander Paine, Janet Parks, James Patterson, Donald Peacock, Jonathan Pepler, Professor Simon Pepper, Sue Poole, Prebendary F. A. Preston, Ismeth Raheem, The Lady Reilly, Sir Patrick Reilly, Mrs A. E. Rice, Margaret Richardson, Peter Richmond, Brian Robson, Francoise Roux, David Rowse, Mr R. J. Saunders, Mr Seagrote, Linda Shaw, Robert S. Shaw, Sir Peter Shepheard, Colin Simpson, Patricia Sloane, George Smith, Jean Smith, Christopher Solomon, Hugh and John Spencely, Joan Stahl, Gavin Stamp, Professor Gordon Stephenson, Damie Stillman, Duncan Stewart, Jane Street, Christina Stringer, Professor J. N. Tarn, Valerie Teague, Jill Temple, Anthony Thearle, the late Mrs V. Thearle, Professor David Thistlewood, Alison Thomas,

Judy Throm, Carol Traynor, Giles Velarde, Peter Wakelin, Carol Willis, Joan Wilson, Mr N. V. Winchester, Fiona Woodward, Dr R. B. Wragg, Brian Wright, Mrs M. Hesketh Wright, Tony Wrenn.

Photographic credits

Avery Architectural and Fine Arts Library, Columbia University in the City of New York: Fig. 74

British Architectural Library, RIBA, London: Figs. 5, 7, 19, 26, 32, 49, 62, 70, 72, 73, 75, 76, 82

Kenneth Broome, Epsom: Fig. 83

Constable Maxwell Photography, Winchester: Fig. 24

Peter Greenhalf, Rye: Figs. 4, 6, 30, 41, 42

The E. Chambré Hardman Trust, Liverpool: Figs. 11, 12, 13, 14, 63, 68, 69

Image, Washington DC: Fig. 36

Merrow Photographers, Guildford: Figs. 8, 10, 76, 77

John Mills, Liverpool: Figs. 1, 3, 9, 15, 20, 33, 37, 39, 43, 45, 46, 47, 50, 51, 52, 55, 58, 78, 81

National Monuments Records for Wales: Figs. 79, 80

National Museums & Galleries on Merseyside, Photography Department: cover, Figs. 35, 38, 40, 48, 64, 65, 66

Joseph Sharples: Fig. 27

University of Liverpool, Central Photographic Service: Figs. 2, 16, 17, 18, 21, 22, 23, 28, 29, 31, 34, 44, 54, 56, 57, 84

Charles Herbert Reilly
Biographical outline, including chief architectural works and publications

1874 Born London, 4 March, son of Charles Reilly (1844–1928), architect and surveyor to the Worshipful Company of Drapers. Educated at Merchant Taylors School and Queens' College, Cambridge. After graduation, works for two years as an unpaid draughtsman in his father's office, then enters the office of John Belcher as an 'improver'.

1898 Associate of the RIBA.

1900 Appointed part-time lecturer in architectural design at King's College, London. Joins in partnership with Stanley Peach, working on the design of electricity generating stations.

1902 Enters Liverpool Cathedral competition.

1904 Appointed Roscoe Professor of Architecture, University of Liverpool.

1905 Designs cottages at Lower Road, Port Sunlight, for William Hesketh Lever.

1906 Invited to join RIBA Board of Architectural Education. Becomes involved as consulting architect in remodelling 'Belmont', near Chesterfiled, for C. B. Ward.

1907 Enters London County Hall competition. Designs Liverpool Students' Union, Ashton Street (not built); garden for Louis Cappel, 5 Ullet Road, Liverpool; and garden for Mr and Mrs J. Reynolds, Dove Park, Woolton.

1909 First visit to America. Department of Civic Design founded within Liverpool School of Architecture. Elected to Council of RIBA. Designs Liverpool Students' Union, Bedford Street/Mount Pleasant, and Church of St Barnabas, Shacklewell, London.

1910 Designs additions to Holy Trinity Church, Wavertree, Liverpool. Begins involvement with founding of Liverpool Repertory Theatre. Leads campaign against altering St George's Hall to accommodate statue of Edward VII.

1911 Appointed Member of Faculty of Architecture, British School at Rome. Publishes designs for Church of Humanity, Liverpool (not built).

1912 Fellow of the RIBA.

1913 Appointed Consulting Editor to the *Builders' Journal*.

1914 Designs new building for Liverpool School of Architecture in Bedford Street (not built).

1915 Begins war work as munitions inspector.

1916 Remodels 8 Buckingham Street, Westminster.

1919 Visits United States and Canada.

1920 Awarded OBE. Visits United States and Canada twice as jury member for Canadian War Memorials competition. Designs Accrington War Memorial, Lancashire.

1921 Publishes *Some Liverpool Streets and Buildings in 1921*. About this time becomes associated with *Country Life* as Architectural Editor.

1923–24 Appointed co-architect, with Thomas Hastings, of Devonshire House, Piccadilly, London. Visits New York. Publishes *McKim, Mead and White*, *Some Architectural Problems of Today*, and *Some Manchester Streets and their Buildings*.

1925 Appointed Corresponding Member of the American Institute of Architects.

1927–28 Travels in India with Lutyens.

1928 Designs Durham War Memorial.

1931 Vice-President of the RIBA, 1931–32. Publishes *Representative Architects of the Present Day*.

1932 Publishes *The Theory and Practice of Architecture*.

1933 Retires as Director of the Liverpool School of Architecture. New School building—the Leverhulme Building—opens, designed by Reilly, Budden and Marshall.

1934 Created Emeritus Professor, University of Liverpool. Begins acting as Consultant Architect with William Crabtree on Peter Jones store, Sloane Square, and John Lewis's, Oxford Street, London.

1935 Co-architect, with L. B. Budden and J. E. Marshall, of extension to Liverpool Students' Union.

1938 Publishes *Scaffolding in the Sky: a semi-architectural autobiography*.

1943 Awarded Royal Gold Medal for Architecture.

1944 Knighted.

1946 Publishes *Architecture as a Communal Art*.

1947 Publishes *Outline Plan for the County Borough of Birkenhead*.

1948 Dies, London, 2 February.

Fig. 1 (Cat. 12) Staff and students of the Liverpool School of Architecture and Applied and Arts. Photograph by Mary 'Bee' Phillips, c.1904. Reilly is in the back row, on the right (The Board of Trustees of the National Museums & Galleries on Merseyside: Walker Art Gallery)

Liverpool and Architectural Education in the Early Twentieth Century

ALAN POWERS

C. H. Reilly's success as a propagandist for the Liverpool School of Architecture and for himself (the two were indistinguishable for a period of thirty years) was so great that the context of his achievement has been largely overlooked. More than any other individual, he was responsible for determining the future shape of architectural education in Britain down to the present, with considerable consequences in the practice of architecture itself. He was a principal actor on a stage of architectural politics and theory in a period that is still not well understood.

There is something symbolic in the commencement of Reilly's professorship soon after the death of Queen Victoria. His enterprise is marked by opposition to Victorian aesthetics, social assumptions and values, symbolised for him at the time by Alfred Waterhouse's Victoria Building in which his teaching commenced in 1904, with 'its colours of mud and blood' and 'glazed tiles the colour of curry powder'. Although the building represented the tardy late Victorian investment in modern municipal university education that was the basis on which Reilly's future school was built, it was, within two years of its completion, conspicuously inappropriate to its place and purpose, coated in soot by the trains passing through the deep cutting on their way to Lime Street.

Reilly was not the first professor of architecture at Liverpool. His predecessor F. M. Simpson was a gentle, scholarly aesthete, an interim figure. His school was representative of the Arts and Crafts Movement which Reilly saw as a partial but insufficient remedy for Victorian failure. Reilly himself was in his thirty-first year when he started work in Waterhouse's building in the middle of 1904. Although a second-generation architect, he was not a well-known name in the architectural world and had not been in practice under his own name. He had good contacts from offices he had worked in. He had some teaching experience from evening classes at King's College, London and a Cambridge degree in engineering which probably impressed the interview panel, as, apparently, did his classical designs for the Liverpool Cathedral competition of 1902, but the other candidates for the post were not strong.[1] Before Reilly demonstrated its potential, a teaching post in architecture was not considered a good career move. His former pupil at King's, S. C. Ramsey, wrote in 1929; 'there were not a few of us who knew and admired

1

Fig. 2 (Cat.5) Perspective by Stanley Adshead of Reilly's 1902 competition design for Liverpool Cathedral (University of Liverpool Art Gallery and Collections)

Reilly in those now far-off days, who rather regretted his acceptance of the Liverpool job'.[2]

Architectural education, such as existed, in the previous decade had been attempting to resolve the divergences of the 'Profession or Art' controversy of 1891 which had arisen in the first place in the vacuum of training and qualification in architecture. The existing arrangements were biased in favour of those who had enough money to buy an articled pupillage (effectively an apprenticeship) in one of the better offices. This was potentially a complete training in itself. After completing the pupillage and graduating to becoming an assistant, a young architect might launch off on his own. In artistic circles, whether connected with church or domestic work of the kind that was particularly admired by foreign visitors such as Hermann Muthesisus, the letters ARIBA, standing for 'Associate of the Royal Institute of British Architects', were not particularly important. This privileged sector of the profession was the one which felt able to boycott the RIBA for at least ten years. Despite his educational advantages, Reilly had not personally followed a straight path into this magic world, so he understood the more gritty alternatives—competition entries, 'ghosting' and 'taking in washing' (freelance draughting and perspective work) which form a perennial underworld of architectural practice. His entry into John Belcher's office was his symbolic passage from the 'profession' to 'art' camps but he seems to have felt that many of those on the art side saw the barrier as part of their own protection and had an inadequate missionary zeal to break down the division or help others across it.

Contrast this with the position of a fourteen-year-old school leaver in Liverpool or Manchester with no personal capital available for education. Work in an architect's office might be available but was more menial and less consciously educational, either by intention or by the rubbing off from the office environment. Free evening classes at a government-funded art or technical school could add technique but were not aimed at culture. The weekly building papers were a lavish source of self-improvement, including design competitions for students. With hard study, such a student might work up to the Associateship exam (available from 1869 and obligatory from 1882), but there would have been no education in the imagination or its application to design apart from what could be picked up by inference or personal contact. The above could be an account of the early career of Charles Holden in Manchester, later one of the most able and individual architects of his generation. Advocates of the status quo could argue that the toughness required for overcoming the inherent defects of such a system was the best qualification for architectural success.

The will to change the system was not easily focused. When action came, it was from outside the RIBA where vested interests induced a virtual paralysis. The profession or art controversy broke out over the question of qualifications for registering architects and denying the title to those not registered. The motive for

3

this came from provincial centres where the status and livelihood of architects was continuously under threat. Design standards were not the uppermost consideration for such architects, to the extent that an examination including design was no more of a stumbling block than one on professional practice or structural mechanics. The RIBA was not itself trying to achieve registration, but was under pressure from a rival body, the Society of Architects, to do so. It probably had the worst of both worlds in the 1890s, losing its support from both sides of the issue, but the election to the presidency of Aston Webb, architect of many public buildings, in 1902 offered the chance to heal the split.

Simpson's appointment to Liverpool in 1894 was an early move in the game by the 'Art' party, represented by Simpson's sponsor, the architect T. G. Jackson. As described in J. M. MacKay's paper 'The teaching of architecture in the new university: a school of the fine arts', there was a favourable background based on the wishes expressed by the retiring Roscoe professor, R. A. M. Stevenson and on the willingness of the local architectural society.[3] Liverpool University (still at this time only a University College) provided an impartial, institutional umbrella, and this model was followed with local variations around the country as locally-funded colleges worked their way upwards to become the 'red brick' universities.

MacKay's own vision was of the University as the leading force in civic culture: 'Through its University Liverpool was to be a new Athens saving the country from its materialism by the clearness of its thought, the fineness of its work and the beauty of its buildings'.[4] This was a continuation of the Unitarian message of civic consciousness as a supplement and, if necessary, alternative to the established church carried over from the early nineteenth century and sustained in Liverpool by great dynasties of non-conformist philanthropists—Holts, Rathbones, Joneses and others who emulated them, such as William Hesketh Lever. This vision of Athens was literally transferable into the architecture of the Greek Revival. MacKay's group of followers and supporters was known as 'The New Testament', and Reilly received every encouragement in expanding the mission of architecture outside the drawing board and into general areas of culture, partly taking the place of the Faculty of Fine Arts which MacKay had hoped to found.

In 1900 architecture had become an honours course in which a BA might be awarded. In 1902 the Degree and Certificate courses were the first to be recognised by the RIBA for exemption from their own Intermediate exam. From these small beginnings grew two of the significant ideas pioneered by Reilly in the first ten years of his office, that architecture might become an academic subject in its own right and that in so doing it would offer a more attractive alternative path towards professional qualification. In other words, through a university training, it became possible to receive a version of both 'profession' and 'art', in terms made acceptable to the RIBA but not directly under its control. A university helped to lift the barriers of class and economics surrounding the architectural profession and open the field for 'art', particularly by allowing access for poorer students on scholar-ships and, after 1919, for women.[5] It also gave a recognisable framework for the training of students from other countries, including India and Egypt, who had previously favoured the courses at University College and King's College, London.

The year 1904 was a critical one in the resolution of the profession or art dispute During the 1890s many interesting experiments were made in training architects according to Arts and Crafts principles, including their participation in trade building classes. The early Liverpool school under Simpson offered training in decorative crafts, as did the evening and day classes at Edinburgh College of Art and Birmingham School of Art. Behind many of these experiments lay the figure of W. R. Lethaby whose ideas of social and artistic reform, based on learning by doing, had influenced the establishment of the London County Council's scheme for technical education in the early 1890s in direct contradiction to the highly structured but paper-based activities of the 'South Kensington system' of the Department of Science and Art whose chief advantage lay in the government funding of its premises and teachers.

In both systems, the underlying assumption was the continuation of architec-tural pupillage as the main means of entry into the profession. The creation of the two-year day course at Liverpool might appear to challenge this but as Reilly explained later, architects still received their premiums in respect of the remaining part of the training and felt relieved of any educational obligations. The idea of achieving exemption from the RIBA exams added further inducement, and a number of day courses began around this time (the AA in 1901, Birmingham in 1902) in order to test the market. One of Aston Webb's actions was to convene an RIBA committee on education and try to bring the active teachers from the 'Art' party, such as Lethaby and Beresford Pite, on to it. The proceedings of this committee, constituted in 1905 as the RIBA Board of Architectural Education, show the point of conflict between Lethaby's ideas and others, espoused and shaped by Reilly, that were to prevail in their place.

In theory, Reilly and Lethaby shared much common ground. Both were searching for a resolution to late Victorian stylistic eclecticism in the belief that too much attention was given to the external features of style and not enough to the extraction of underlying principles of architecture and structure. They both rejected Art Nouveau or its derivatives as a possible solution because they believed it to be irrational. They sought abstraction combined with an openness to new building techniques rather than a break with the past. They were also both concerned over a long period with the aesthetic and political issues of the public realm in architecture, an issue which the laissez-faire policies of both political parties tended to ignore. The focus of attention for architects had for many years been the individual building, but the condition of late Victorian cities, smoke-blackened, with poor transport and circulation, demonstrated that the neglect of larger issues was making even this isolated method of practice untenable. Their suggested means were, however, very different.

Lethaby came to the first meeting of the RIBA committee with a proposal which resembled his schemes for the LCC, including an extensive 'Laboratory of Building'. There were to be graded steps of inductive learning, based on positivistic knowledge of materials. History, aesthetics and design were virtually excluded. This was one way of curing eclecticism, but Lethaby's own close colleagues like Beresford Pite had already told him that it was too severe and idealistic. Since 1900 much had changed in the temper of the times and taste was developing away from the abstraction of arts and crafts design, represented by C. F. A. Voysey, towards simpler and more refined versions of the historical styles.

Reilly's initial achievement was to grasp that classicism could be a path to abstraction, and furthermore one which offered educational advantages on many levels. He was led partly by personal predilection (as demonstrated in his Liverpool Cathedral designs which defied the Gothic requirement of the competition conditions), partly by an awakening feeling for the architectural *genius loci* of Liverpool.

The 'Applied Arts' as taught at Liverpool during Simpson's regime might well have failed to satisfy Lethaby's standards for vocational craft training, since apart from Augustus John's drawing tuition in the period 1901–03 they were involved more with modelling and decorative metalwork than building crafts. The action which divorced them from the architecture course was one of financial reallocation by the municipal funding authorities, although Herbert McNair, Charles Rennie Mackintosh's brother-in-law, and the painter Gerald Chowne preferred not to teach in the town art school under the South Kensington system and for a few years ran an independent art school. In the process, Augustus John also ceased his association with Liverpool. The closure of the 'Art Sheds' certainly enabled Reilly to focus the architectural school and make a clean sweep of the old regime.

Reilly's alternative course was not immediately formulated. Then, as now, there were scruples about the open adoption of classical style even though it was a common feature of current architectural practice. In the early twentieth century, such scruples arose partly from a lingering respect for Ruskin's condemnation of the renaissance that made correct classicism seem illicit, partly from a sense that English architecture was special and valuable because of its individuality and freedom, fostered by pupillage. Reilly's inaugural lecture managed to steal the enemies clothes on a number of points. He stressed the English character of Georgian architecture and argued in broad terms for the quality of decorum in Georgian houses and furniture, cleverly introducing a note of local patriotism in mentioning that 'there were in Liverpool many old houses, not unlike those in Bath, containing beautiful antique work' which students would measure and draw.[6] For London, this would not have been an exceptional attitude, but it contrasted with Simpson's complaint a few years earlier that Liverpool did not contain suitable old buildings for study.[7] Reilly briefly sketched the concern with town planning as the counterpart of architecture and was also able to annex the doctrine of the Arts and Crafts movement in recalling 'the union of architecture and sculpture' which he claimed as part of the English tradition.

Reilly was quick to grasp the interconnected advantages that a classical training could bring. It was a defined body of doctrine which made architectural design into a teachable subject with standards of comparability for examination. This he saw as a *sine qua non* of university status and a sufficient compensation for the questionable benefits of individualism. 'It might be laid down as an axiom that early teaching in any art to be effective must be academic. A convention must be assumed, and, more than that, it must be accepted as an article of faith. That alone will make the school into a living organism'.[8] It could be validated by international standards, particularly those of France and America, countries then politically ascendant from the British viewpoint where architectural education had a longer and more consistent record. The American example was particularly important. It was only around 1905 that Britain began to recognise the work of the American classical movement that had been current since the design of McKim Mead and White's Boston Public Library in 1887 and by 1900 had become the dominant style for education and practice. Liverpool's position as the main port for America made a symbolic connection supported by personal and business links. Reilly's most visionary skill was in recreating an image of Liverpool as a great neo–classical city. The arguments about architectural individuality and national character were self-evidently limiting in the face of a building of international stature such as St George's Hall.

Reilly shared with others of his generation a feeling that the picturesque movement of the nineteenth century had replaced clear thinking by sentimentality, with effects that damaged the relationship of architectural design to construction and introduced inappropriate aesthetic qualities into the public realm. This belief influenced the graphic style of the school, where elevations rendered with conventionalised shadows were preferred to perspectives. The thickly ruled lines normal in competition drawings were replaced by more delicate draughtsmanship. Texture in buildings which was one of the prized qualities of the Arts and Crafts movement became of little account. Design subjects were nearly always urban. Originality in detail was not prized; instead Reilly used new castings of late Georgian and Regency cast iron details in his Liverpool Students' Union building. In the School of Civic Design, the anti-picturesque doctrine was operated most tellingly against the advocates of Garden City planning.

Had Reilly looked to the Netherlands or Germany, he could have found alternative traditions of architectural teaching less closely linked to a particular

Fig. 4 (Cat. 65) Photograph by Stewart Bale of the interior of the Gilmour Hall, Liverpool University Students' Union, designed by Reilly (Courtesy of Eric and Joanna Le Fevre)

Fig. 3 (Cat. 67) Church of St Barnabas, Shacklewell, designed by Reilly, opened 1910. Reproduced in *The Book of the Liverpool School of Architecture*, 1932.

style. These, in his view, would probably have been tainted with Art Nouveau. Following the lead of the American classicists, Reilly and other British admirers of the Ecole des Beaux Arts in Paris misinterpreted what they saw as being a system based on classicism, rather than a rationalist system whose principal manifestations were classical. The difference may seem subtle, but is nonetheless crucial, for as the Liverpool School developed under Reilly the specific style he liked to call 'Monumental Classic' became an end in itself rather than the means to the abstract end that it had been at the outset. In his own design work, the contrast can be made between the church of St Barnabas, Shacklewell (1908–10) which effectively exemplifies the doctrine of abstract form derived from classicism, and the Liverpool University Student Union in which abstract form is overlaid with excessive ornament of uncertain quality.

The difference between the English version of the Beaux Arts and the French is seen in the contrast between Liverpool under Reilly and the Glasgow School of Architecture under Professor Eugene Bourdon, also appointed in 1904, the only genuine French teacher operating in the British system before 1913. As the hybrid monster of the English Beaux Arts began to form under Reilly's spell, Bourdon did his best to warn that 'these teachers, these missionaries from Paris, must be careful to bear in mind that it is not French art and styles that we want to have introduced here [i.e. in Glasgow], but the old Greek, Roman and Italian methods of studying architecture, yet improved by the French gift for clearness and order'.[9]

The fundamental difference between the Ecole des Beaux Arts and the British schools of architecture was in their respective institutional structures. The Ecole was funded by the government and offered centralised facilities for formal teaching and examination. Studio teaching was conducted in private ateliers run by distinguished architects and was only institutionalised in so far as conformity was needed to achieve sufficient grades to pass through the school, something that students expected to take several years in doing. The Atelier combined some of the personal qualities of pupillage without its risk of counter-educational exploitation. The French system was a pyramid, capped by the Grand Prix de Rome, beyond which lay a reasonable assurance of official patronage. In the English system, government funding was thinly spread and there was no desire to make the architecture course of the Royal College of Art, the only one funded by the government, into a central establishment. Institutions were jealous of power and influence and felt that pupillage was the main rival attraction for students' funds and time and therefore necessarily the enemy.

However much Reilly and his English colleagues professed to admire the Ecole at this time, the American system of big university schools of architecture offered a more attractive structure in which students were carefully channelled and controlled. America offered examples of professional competence in design, office procedure, innovative steel frame construction and contracting which were evident in London in Selfridges by Daniel H. Burnham, begun in 1908, and in buildings of the 1920s including Devonshire House where Reilly was associated with the New York architect Thomas Hastings. Reilly made use of his 1909 trip to the States to make contacts for work-experience placements for his students.

Reilly's command of the media may also have owed something to American models. It certainly became symbiotic with the School's development. For publicity purposes a school working on inductive methods, leaving students to find their own answers, was no use. Clear doctrines, supported by clear drawings were needed and these must be brought before the professional public and, when possible, the non-professional public.

The *Liverpool Portfolio of Measured Drawings*, of which two numbers were produced in 1906 and 1908, followed a tradition of 'Sketchbooks' of measured drawings but the Liverpool books, without displaying any outstanding graphic skill, showed a new taste for later and more correct classical buildings, whether in Britain or abroad. The components of the 'Monumental Classic' pantheon are already apparent in the drawings of C. R. Cockerell's Bank of England branch in Castle Street, Liverpool, details of St George's Hall and St Paul's Church, linked with the Palazzo Bevilacqua and the Porta Palio in Verona. Drawings by students were regularly published in the architectural papers of the time, but Reilly tried to ensure that his students' work was well-represented and reproduced in half-tone on art paper. Having collected together a group of blocks, he was able to launch the publication of the *Liverpool Architectural Sketchbook* in 1910 through Technical Journals Ltd, the publishers of the weekly *Builders' Journal* (later *Architects' Journal*) of which Reilly himself became deputy editor in 1913. The sketchbooks were published again in 1911 and 1913, with one final issue after the war in 1920, but through the *Builders Journal* Reilly established links with like-minded architects in London such as Albert Richardson. He was not afraid to criticise an established figure such as Norman Shaw over his proposals to alter the plinth of St George's Hall in 1910–11, seeing in this issue a focus of the differences between the old picturesque generation and his own generation's greater respect for civic decorum. Reilly was undoubtedly intemperate in this affair, but the abiding feeling is his need symbolically to kill off the old king and begin a new regime. The same impulse surrounded the attempt to raise controversy over the award to Ralph Knott of the London County Hall in 1908, a competition which Reilly himself had entered, as had S. D. Adshead. Norman Shaw and Aston Webb were the assessors (both, incidentally, had written references for Reilly's application for the professorship). The issues were that civic building could no longer be judged on picturesque principles but demanded a more serious consideration of programme and appropriateness of form.

The year 1909 was important in the development of the School. Through the involvement of W. H. Lever (later Lord Leverhulme), Reilly was able to announce the foundation of the Department of Civic Design, invite his friend Stanley Adshead to apply for the Professorship and travel to America, ostensibly to gather material for the new department while visiting many schools of architecture. Lever's munificence also provided the School with a fitting new home in the Bluecoat Chambers, renamed Liberty Buildings. These achievements were subtly interconnected in their enlargement of the scope of architecture into the civic realm of town planning and as an example of conservationist intervention and what would later be called adaptive re-use. The selection of Adshead made clear that the intention of the Civic Design school was to consider the aesthetic aspects of town planning as an extension of architecture. The transfer of Patrick Abercrombie who from 1907 was a lecturer in the architecture school to the new department, was responsible for his future professional direction, with far-reaching consequences for British cities. In securing Lever's funding for the *Town Planning Review*, Reilly again displayed his instinct for publicity and dissemination of ideas.

In 1910, Reginald Blomfield became Chairman of the RIBA Board of Architectural Education and was lobbied by Reilly. After the initial discussions in 1904–05, the Board had quietly let most of Lethaby's proposals fade away. Reilly had no desire to concede it greater power, writing to H. P. G. Maule, the head of the AA School in 1906: 'The Board is not an executive body to my mind but only an advisory one. They approve or disapprove of our actions. If we let them go further we may find ourselves when a new lot of men get on it with a kind of South Kensington and if you have had anything to do with running an art school you will know what a deadening thing that is'.[10] The issue before the Board was the creation of a Diploma in architecture, awarded after two further years of evening classes and thus permitting the schools to retain their pupils longer and produce more sophisticated work. At this point, any opposition to the primacy of design study in teaching died and the culminating work of a student's career was proposed as a 'thesis design' resembling as closely as possible the work of a practising architect.

Reilly was shaping a course, which effectively disarmed those on the Board like Lethaby who no longer were, however strongly they disapproved of what he was doing. Had the Board been more resolute about sticking to a Lethabite programme, it might have been possible to withhold exam exemption from Liverpool until it conformed, but this would have been politically explosive and presumably no-one felt able to risk another split so soon after 'Profession or Art'. Even Lethaby did not have the full support of his associates such as Pite. Reilly was able with little effort to ensure that the other schools broadly followed his lead. In the case of the Architectural Association, he was able to stir up opposition to the teaching methods of Maule to the extent that he resigned in 1912. This is one of Reilly's least creditable episodes. Maule had good reason for resisting what he referred to as 'selective shirt-front architecture'[11] on Beaux Arts principles while Reilly managed to promote a caricature version of the AA as a school where young gentlemen designed cottages and pig sties, which was far from the truth. The result was that by 1912 no substantial alternative to the 'Liverpool style' seemed available and Blomfield overcame his personal doubts about a classicism of rules and presided over adjustments to the exam syllabus. Reilly set design programmes for the new diploma exam which virtually demanded a treatment in the manner he had promoted.

The last years before the First World War saw the sketching in of a broader institutional structure in architectural education which validated what Liverpool had begun. In 1912 it was proposed to turn the British School at Rome into the equivalent of the other foreign academies which offered scholarships to outstanding young painters, sculptors and architects.[12] It was a rare moment when official support for art seemed politically possible and was in a wider sense the culmination of long-lasting attempts to gain for art and architecture a recognised place in national life. By the selection of a Rome Scholar each year (a runner-up prize, the Henry Jarvis scholarship, was also awarded), a cadre of scholarly designers would be established for the benefit of the public realm. This orderly procedure in each of the arts would seem to redeem them from the accusation of being unpredictable and subversive activities unsuitable for state support. The results too often looked as if all the life had been squeezed out of them.

Reilly was a member of the Faculty of Architecture from the outset and collaborated with Lethaby in setting the design briefs, 'An Art Gallery' for the intial open competition and 'A City Centre or Modern Forum surrounded by important public buildings' for the final competition. Heads of recognised architectural schools were also allowed to nominate candidates for the final competition. Something like the Ecole system was adopted with an 'esquisse en loge', a sketch design under exam conditions, setting the main outlines of the scheme which would be developed over a month in a grand series of rendered elevations, plans and sections. The final competition, in the early years, was carried out entirely under supervision in London in conditions far from ideal. Reilly complained in 1924: 'It was the want of fresh air more the thirty-six hours work which did for some of my boys before'.[13] He also characteristically suggested that the candidates should be rewarded with a dinner at the end at which members of the Faculty could meet them informally.

The skills required to win the scholarship were exactly those that Reilly had fostered since 1904. No knowledge of construction needed to be displayed and originality of detail was severely penalised. It was the triumph of drawing over building, but the sanctity of the Beaux Arts tradition placed it almost beyond criticism. It was not surprising that the first winner was a Liverpool student Harold Chalton Bradshaw who had been the slide projectionist before Reilly found scholarships for him to take the course. Bradshaw completed the buildings of the

British School at Rome begun by Lutyens and designed war memorials with sculpture by other Rome scholars, Gilbert Ledward and Charles Sargent Jagger. On his appointment as first secretary of the Royal Fine Art Commission in 1923 he ceased to practise architecture. Other distinguished Liverpool scholars followed, notably W. G. Holford (1930) who married the painting scholar of the same year, Marjorie Brooks. That Holford became famous as an administrator and com-mittee-man rather than as a creative architect typifies the stultifying effect of the scholarship. Several became architectural teachers, including Stephen Welsh, who was at Rome when Reilly reported back from a visit to the school in 1924: 'The students did me very well giving me a dance in my honour and dressing me up for the occasion. The famous Miss Knights was there to be married next day to one of the painters'.[14] Reilly's interest in the other scholarship winners extended to organising the commission for Edward Halliday (Painting Scholar 1925) to execute three panels of mythological subjects for the Library of the Athenaeum opposite the Bluecoat School, a building by a pre-war Liverpool student Harold Dod.

The Great War came too soon for a pattern of public patronage of Rome Scholars to become established. Immediately after the war Reilly approached the Ministry of Works which refused to give any preferential treatment to them. All he was able to achieve was a scheme whereby Lloyds Bank employed the scholars to build branch banks on their return from Rome. The danger was realised early on that two or three years in Rome might, despite the prestige of the scholarship, be detrimental to career prospects. Reilly also came to regret the confining of

Fig. 5 The Basilica of Constantine, actual state elevation to Via Sacra, 1927. Drawn by Charles Anthony Minoprio while a student at the British School at Rome. Cf cat. 39 and 40. (British Architectural Library, RIBA, London)

scholarship work to the survey and conjectural restoration of ancient monuments in Rome in the French tradition when the candidates were selected on the basis of design ability. In fact, the Rome scholarship became one way in which the ideas of continental modernism entered British architecture, an opposite outcome to the strengthening of the classical tradition which the founders such as Blomfield intended, but one which may not have distressed Reilly by the end of the 1920s.

Less official in status than the Rome School was the First Atelier which opened in London in 1913 under the auspices of the Society of Architects. Effectively it was like an evening design club such as had flourished intermittently before the institutionalisation of architectural education, but again it suggested that the Beaux Arts method could recapture the spontaneity and camaraderie of an earlier period, even if not quite the studio atmosphere of Paris itself. Reilly welcomed it and imagined a network of ateliers interlocking with the institutional schools.

By the outbreak of the First World War, Reilly had developed his programme at the Liverpool School to a remarkable extent and made it the paradigm for a newly created national hierarchy of architectural education. It was not a deeply-based achievement and the student drawings look inadequate in terms of design and presentation compared with the work of French and American student work. The adoption of classicism favoured a superficial approach to design which failed to engage in the new technical aspects of architecture. Referring to this, Reilly declared in a letter to Sir Giles Scott of 20 December 1942,: 'The Liverpool fellows in my time did all go through the discipline of classical architecture. Except for the precision of its rules, I wish now it had been Gothic, for Gothic with its constructional basis is much nearer to modern stuff with its steel and ferro-concrete.'

The First World War fell like a cesura in Reilly's career. Reilly himself was away from the School on war service and its activities diminished. The School lost its distinguished home in the former Bluecoat School and moved into 'Reilly's cowshed', a range of condemned hospital buildings which seem in fact to have lent themselves well to the purpose. His later period at Liverpool, from 1919 to 1933, could be seen as the second act of a tragedy, in which the hero learns the consequences of defying the gods, those values over which he had so gleefully trampled as a young man. We have his letter to Scott as partial evidence that he might have shared this view, and the evidence of his own apparent rejection in the later 1920s of the architectural style on which he had built the School's reputation.

The common view in the past has been that Reilly's lack of awareness of European proto-modernism in the pre-1914 period implicated him in the thirty wasted years between the completion of Glasgow School of Art and the construction of the Boots D10 building by Owen Williams in 1930, a period in which the whole effort of architectural education and culture was brusquely rendered irrelevant by an engineer. This view identifies the future modern style

14

and traces its gradual and inevitable dissemination around the world. To concentrate on America, as Reilly did so emphatically in the 1920s, was arguably to unbalance English architecture by denying the more romantic influences then coming strongly from Scandinavia and northern Europe, let alone the intellectual roots of modern architecture which were exclusively European. This seems to have been the feeling of Charles Rennie Mackintosh who gave his opinion in 1927 that the American system was wrong, and that Reilly did not even reproduce it effectively.[15]

The ethos of Liverpool in the 1920s remained classical, although it was possible through the Beaux Arts method to retain the principles and change the details towards a cooler or perhaps more Art Deco character, as found in the work of one of Reilly's most successful local pupils Herbert J. Rowse. This transition was typical of the work of French Beaux Arts-trained architects and of those who had studied in Paris such as Raymond Hood or the French-Canadian Ernest Cormier. At the same time, Reilly perpetuated the sense of fun with which he had refreshed the solemnity of the late Edwardian period. He encouraged fantasy projects as sketch designs to develop technique, writing that 'Every Tuesday morning the sketch designs of the previous Monday from each year were hung up and, after a jury of teachers, including myself, had assessed them, I generally gave the criticism. Indeed, I made a point of giving it to the early years. They are generally the important ones on which to make an impression. It is with them that the imagination most easily catches fire. The designs themselves must, of course, be of an imaginative kind. The hard geometrical work, architecture in the solid, goes on all the week. Mondays were for architecture in the clouds. I believe that is laughed at today, but it produced results. Palaces for Kubla Khan are in my opinion a necessary part of architectural education'.[16]

Although effective as an antidote to the dryness of Beaux Arts classicism, Reilly's flights of the imagination could not develop into a viable alternative method. In Britain generally there was considerable scepticism about European modernism which Reilly condemned in 1925 for 'consciously trying to create a new style out of thin air'.[17] He was not personally disposed to admire a building such as Stockholm Town Hall by Ostberg which opened in 1923 and inspired many of the English with the prospect of a freely composed romantic architecture as an alternative to classicism. Yet as with many of his contemporaries Reilly became aware that aspects of 1920s classicism were becoming untenable, either through the trivialisation of imagery or through the mismatch between structure and applied facing. This was the view of one of Reilly's favourite pupils Maxwell Fry, who recalled seeing Devonshire House under construction (the year would then have been 1925) with its renaissance cherubs: 'I knew it all like a game played out, and in those duplicating amorini, the last of their long line, I thought to find the cherubic face of my naughty professor playing Ariel to old man Hastings in

Fig. 6 (Cat. 30) A Baldacchino, six-hour sketch design by Derek Bridgwater, early 1920s (Courtesy of Eric and Joanna Le Fevre)

New York and turned in a gesture of moral revulsion from everything I had been taught'.[18] Fry's rejection of his Liverpool training was as radical as he could make it, but appears not to have happened at least until 1932 and he was content for his early neo-Georgian work to be published in *The Book of the Liverpool School of Architecture* in that year.

If Modernism was an inevitable development, then Reilly can be said to have managed the change skilfully and productively. In the words of an anonymous editorial writer in the *Architects' Journal*, 'The chasm between Devonshire House and Peter Jones is a big one—for many of our friends and neighbours a bottomless pit—but it is typical of Professor Reilly that he has leapt it, or perhaps it would be truer to say that he has waved the chasm aside with a noble gesture and, behold, there is no longer a chasm'.[19] For the Peter Jones store Reilly was named as a consultant with his former student William Crabtree, working in a style recognisably derived from Mendelsohn if adapted for English consumption. It was some achievement to be associated with the one modern building of the 1930s which has presented no problems of structure and maintenance and has remained perennially popular with its clientele who might be considered among those least likely to approve of it. Reilly used a photograph of it for the cover of his autobiography.

Mendelsohn lectured at Liverpool three weeks after his arrival in England in 1933. His influence was incompatible with specific Beaux Arts methods of axial symmetry, although being based on aesthetic ideas of composition it was a comparable alternative. Within the school, a change seems to have been led by the students, as recalled by Sir Peter Shepheard: 'We threw away our watercolours and started going to Germany and doing line drawings'. His final year thesis design was of shining blocks of ten-storey flats in the style of Le Corbusier, and although this was in 1936, the change had begun in Reilly's last two years. Commenting on the end of year show in 1932, Wesley Dougill remarked how 'much of the success of the Liverpool School depends on the thorough grounding in traditional forms which the students receive in the earlier years of the course. It is not until they have reached the latter half of the third year that their work is preponderatingly modern. Thus there is a virtual absence of half-baked designs carried out in a style which at once presupposes a scientific and advanced knowledge of construction and materials, a knowledge which junior students cannot possibly have attained to'.[20] Myles Wright recognised in Maxwell Fry's modernist work the benefits of a classical formation, writing in 1937: 'I have always felt privately that Mr Fry was one of the few British architects who are completely masters of his treacherous modern business. I now suspect that Liverpool has something to do with it; even that Professor Reilly may be behind it all'.[21]

Reilly's generation divided among themselves in their attitudes to architectural modernism. Some, like Howard Robertson, the head of the Architectural Association, felt able to normalise it as an extension of their previous teaching but

Fig. 7 (Cat. 134) William Crabtree, with Charles Reilly and Slater & Moberly: Peter Jones store, Sloane Square, London, 1935–39. (British Architectural Library, RIBA, London)

Fig. 8 Peter Jones store under construction (British Architectural Library, RIBA, London)

left to his successors the difficult resolution of modernism's more demanding agenda of research-based design study in collaborative groups. This was the issue over which H. S. Goodhart-Rendel defended the Beaux Arts insistence on graphic skills and individual design work in 1938 and lost. These issues were never in dispute at Liverpool where the look of the designs changed without alteration to the structure of the courses. The process of learning the classical orders became a symbol of any school's attitude. They survived until Reilly's retirement, were then dropped but reinstated by John Brandon-Jones when teaching the first year at the end of the 1930s on the pretext that they made a good exercise in accurate drawing and observation. Professor Albert Richardson at the Bartlett School was notable in resisting the influence of modernism altogether, although willing to allow a degree of abstraction within the classical formulae of composition.

Fry's rejection of his classical training included a rejection of the labour-intensive drawings for major competitions and the unrealistic nature of the programmes implied in them. The new ethos was inclined to be puritanical, in contrast to Reilly's encouragement of colour and fun in the 1920s. S. C. Ramsey commented in 1933 on the danger that 'we shall all drift into a dull acceptance of some easy and facile rendering of a mechanised civilisation'.[22] The structures of the national system of education were actually by then so rooted that they absorbed modernism rather than the other way round, and by the 1950s it was clear that modern architecture had become for many an alternative version of the Beaux Arts.

In the inadequate formulation of the meaning and potential of modern architecture came the nemesis of the Edwardian pride in assuming that fine drawings could substitute for what Lethaby, writing to the Sheffield architect Charles Hadfield about the condition of architectural education, called 'hard training and drill and discipline'.[23] In an earlier letter, Lethaby had warned that 'architecture in England having escaped the "Scylla" of Registration may ere long be landed on "Charybdis" and fall body and soul into the hands of the schoolmasters . . . [who] at the present time are doing their best by training a race of architectural prigs to strangle great and dignified architecture'.[24] There can be no doubt that Reilly was the chief target of this statement and it had some truth. There was no self-evident superiority in the work of pupils trained at Liverpool or any other school. There was no guarantee of getting a good job at the end of it, as Lawrence Wright's animated film, *The Life and Career of Archie Teck*, humorously pointed out.

In Reilly's early years classicism had gone beyond being an educational means and had become an end in itself. He could be said to have got back on his own original course after a long deviation and merely shared in the apparent suspension of architectural development during the greater part of the 1920s, but it is questionable whether, stripped of the specifics of ornament, the principles of pure composition left enough to sustain a satisfactory architecture. He was not immune

19

from the tendency of English architecture to prefer styles to principles and to find in modernism a useful style. Liverpool might have given more attention to modern constructional techniques and their implications for design and thus have evolved a modernism of greater depth, instead of which student work and executed designs could be unbelievably dull. The ease with which the classical trappings were discarded suggests that no profound meaning or expressive power had been discovered in them despite a twenty-five-year concerted effort. The same criticisms would be general ones within architectural education. The staffing of the School by its own former pupils tended to be incestuous and rather than design great buildings, many of the most academically successful students and Rome Scholars became teachers themselves, never with the same flair as Reilly himself.

By the late 1940s when another post-war generation was in the School under the tutelage of Reilly's successor, Lionel Budden, the lightly-modernised Beaux Arts curriculum was the cause of further rebellion. The generation which included James Stirling and was taught by Colin Rowe found the general blandness unbearable and used the resources of Liverpool's own architecture, as well as the example of Le Corbusier, to develop an alternative. Stirling recalled: 'Renderings were executed on stretched Whatman paper, flood-washes were used and graded shadows were normal. In the first year we did full colour compositions of the classical orders.' Stirling felt in retrospect that the Beaux Arts and the Bauhaus, both architectural systems derived from pedagogic practice, 'are for us now equally unfortunate. There surely must be another way driving down between them'.[25]

Reilly's life was not circumscribed by his School and we must look to his wider achievements to redeem the limitations of formal architectural teaching. Reilly was a great communicator in a world where architecture was still an interest almost wholly confined to its own professionals. As a writer his easy pluralism was an asset and through articles in *Country Life*, the *Listener*, the *Manchester Guardian* and the *Banker* he was able to develop a new public. In the professional press he was prepared to comment, summarise and formulate where others feared to tread, notably in his series of annual summaries of the previous year's buildings in the *Architects' Journal* from 1926 onwards. Although much about inter-war architecture may appear irredeemably mediocre, Reilly's commentaries do much to render it comprehensible and he resisted the temptation to equate quality with any particular style.

Reilly's grasp of the importance of the public and political aspects of architecture inspired his pupils and if their talents were largely lost to design, at least H. C. Bradshaw as the First Secretary of the Royal Fine Art Commission and W. G. Holford as a consummate post-war architectural politician were able to make a case for architecture in a wider world. Reilly was effective in making architecture part of general culture, encouraging painters and sculptors to play a part in buildings and introducing literary figures to architecture and vice versa. If the conservation movement is considered one of the distinctive and valuable features of English architectural culture in the later twentieth century, Reilly could be said to have laid some if its foundations. His insistence on the character of cities and the need to continuously improve and remake them left an equivocal legacy. Would Liverpool have been a better place if no planner had ever been near it? Nonetheless Colin Rowe as a young teacher was able to draw renewed inspiration from the City of Liverpool and communicate it to his pupils Robert Maxwell and James Stirling with far-reaching results including his own ultimate rejection of the basic myths of modernism.

Reilly's professorship finished in the years between the first and second Architects' Registration Acts, in which the 'Profession or Art' controversy was finally resolved because there were architectural schools which commanded a sufficient consensus of approval within the profession to provide the basis for qualification. Registration was concordant with Reilly's vision of an architecture of public service rather than of individualism. The concerns of registration were still as incompatible with artistic and imaginative quality as they had been in 1891, however, and the success of one system of training rendered impossible the

Fig. 9 Reilly—seated, in centre—at what is probably the 1912 Oriental fancy dress dance of the Sandon Studios Society (Courtesy of Professor Stanley Adshead's grandchildren)

development of any others, as post-war experience showed. Nearly a century after Reilly's professorship began, the institutional structures of architectural education which he was chiefly influential in developing remain in place. It still seems difficult to teach design without at least a tacit agreement about a dominant style, which is thereby likely to be accorded an excessive value. The separation of architectural education from real life is an unavoidable aspect of school-based training and imposes limits on the depth of study. The conclusion of Jules Lubbock and Mark Crinson's study of architectural education in Britain, *Architecture, art or profession?* (1994) is that the Beaux Arts system underlay what they describe as 'The Modernist Academy' which they believe to be outdated in its turn.

Viewed against this background, Reilly is an ambiguous figure. He created and served a system that stood for much that, on a personal level, he disagreed with. His human qualities which come so strongly through all accounts of him were saving graces in a period when architecture seemed in danger of losing much of its humanity.

Notes

1 In *Scaffolding in the Sky*, Reilly wrote that 'later I was to hear that an American architect had been my chief competitor' (p. 67). This was E. Lorch (MA Harvard), Assistant Professor of Architecture at the Drexel Institute, Philadelphia. See *Liverpool University Council Reports* I, p. 29, meeting of 16 February 1904, Liverpool University Archives.

2 S. C. Ramsey, 'An Architect of the Invisible', *Architects' Journal*, 20 March 1929, p. 470.

3 J. M. MacKay, 'The Teaching of Architecture in the New University: A School of the Fine Arts, delivered to the Architectural Society of Liverpool', in *A Miscellany, presented to John Macdonald MacKay, Ll.D.*, Liverpool, 1914, pp. 355–62.

4 C. H. Reilly, *Scaffolding in the Sky*, 1938, p. 77.

5 The earliest woman to receive the certificate in architecture was Eunice Dora Blackwell in 1920. She married the Liverpool-trained architect Clifford Holliday. The Architectural Association first admitted women students in 1917 to help fill places during the First World War.

6 C. H. Reilly, 'Some Tendencies in Modern Architecture', *British Architect*, 12 May 1905, p. 329.

7 In his description of the course ('University College, Liverpool', *Architectural Review*, XIV, 1903, p. 88) Simpson wrote, 'visits are also occasionally paid to workshops and to old buildings of interest but unfortunately not many of the latter exist in or near Liverpool'.

8 C. H. Reilly, 'Architecture as an Academic Subject', op. cit. in note 3, p. 12.

9 Eugene Bourdon, 'The Training of Architects on Beaux-Arts Lines', *Society of Architects Journal*, 1912–13, p. 164.

10 Reilly to Maule, 15 October 1906, Reilly letter book, Liverpool University Archives D207/2/1.

11 H. P. G. Maule, 'Architectural Education, a plea for breadth and sanity', *RIBA Journal*, 1912, p. 342.

12 Reilly had anticipated this move by arranging for the winner of the W. Jones

Travelling Scholarship in 1910, Ernest Prestwich, to be associated with the British School (then housed on the second floor of the Palazzo Odaleschi without residential facilities). He wrote to the school secretary, Baker-Penoyre, 'I should very much like the outcome of the scholarship to be a set of drawings of some monumental building of antiquity which we should not be ashamed to compare with those produced by the French at the Villa Medici'. Reilly to Baker-Penoyre, 21 January 1911, Reilly letter book, Liverpool University Archives, S3205.

13 Reilly to Evelyn Shaw, Secretary of the British School at Rome, 19 March 1924, BSR archives, box 232.

14 Reilly to Evelyn Shaw, 7 May 1924, loc. cit. Winifrid Knights married W. T. Monnington (later Sir Thomas Monnington PRA) on 23 April 1923.

15 Letter from C. R. Mackintosh to his wife, quoted in Roger Bilcliffe, Mackintosh Watercolours, 1978, p. 20.

16 Op. cit. in note 4, pp. 208–09.

17 C. H. Reilly, 'Recent American Architecture', *Architects' Journal*, 29 April 1925, p. 648.

18 Maxwell Fry, *Autobiographical Sketches*, 1975, p. 136.

19 *Architects' Journal*, 21 October 1937, p. 609.

20 Wesley Dougill, 'Work of the Schools: Liverpool', *Architects' Journal*, 6 July 1932, p. 12.

21 H. Myles Wright, 'The Work of the Liverpool School', *Architects' Journal*, 29 May 1937, p. 848.

22 S. C. Ramsey, 'Charles Herbert Reilly' in *The Book of the Liverpool School of Architecture*, 1932, p. 28.

23 Lethaby to Hadfield, 10 June 1907, RIBA Hadfield MSS 83.

24 *RIBA Special Committee Minutes 1899–1908*, p. 256.

25 James Stirling, 'Reflections on the Beaux Arts', *Architectural Design*, XLVIII, Nos 11–12, 1978, p. 88.

Reilly and his Students, on Merseyside and Beyond

JOSEPH SHARPLES

Stirrat Johnson-Marshall (1912–81) was an eighteen-year old schoolboy when he came under the influence of Reilly's extraordinary magnetism. It was 1930 and he was travelling to Manchester by train for an interview to study Civil Engineering when 'a plump gentleman got into the compartment wearing a black coat and broad-brimmed hat. This gentleman engaged him in discussion and persuaded him that architecture was his real mission, and that he should accompany him to Liverpool for an interview with the Professor, who was none other than the plump gentleman, Sir Charles Reilly'.[1] In the end, the quality of a school depends on the quality of its students, and for almost thirty years Reilly ensured the pre-eminence of the Liverpool School of Architecture by attracting, nurturing and rewarding talented students, and by grooming them for future success. Stirrat Johnson-Marshall went on to become chief architect to the Ministry of Education and a key player in the field of public architecture after the Second World War; his achievements were not untypical among the top flight of 'Reilly's young men'.

During Reilly's time at Liverpool the annual intake of students rose steadily, from eleven in 1904 to forty-eight in 1932.[2] The increase in numbers was accompanied by a broadening of the School's constituency. Ten of the eleven new students of 1904 had come from Liverpool or Merseyside, but in 1932 locals were easily outnumbered by those from elsewhere in the country and from overseas.

It is difficult to know the social background of these students. Some may have fitted Lionel Esher's rather waspish description of the successful 1930s architect, trained under the old system of articled pupillage: 'a mildly artistic boy from one of the "minor" public schools . . . With his gift for drawing he would have been steered by his parents, themselves probably professional people, into this gentleman's profession in which mediocrity would matter less than in Art'.[3] Certainly a significant number were from public schools. W. Naseby Adams (Cert. Arch. 1906), a vicar's son from Everton, held the somewhat exclusive view that 'it is the sensitive gentlemen who alone can produce architecture; others just build',[4] and Reilly could display a snobbish pride in having attracted students from privileged backgrounds.[5]

But throughout Reilly's period the School provided opportunities for those

Fig. 10 Reilly with colleagues and senior students, probably late 1920s. The framed drawings in the background include Reilly's designs for the Accrington War Memorial, Liverpool Cathedral and the Students' Union (British Architectural Library, RIBA, London)

whose origins were less affluent. To take one example, Sidney Colwyn Foulkes, born in 1884, was the son of a bankrupt builder and had been his family's breadwinner from the age of sixteen. Having built up a small local practice in Colwyn Bay he attended the School from 1914 to 1916 with the aid of a scholarship, and went on to an outstandingly successful career in North Wales.[6] Remembering the basement room in the Bluecoat building where Reilly lectured on architectural history, Foulkes later recalled: 'that cellar to me was a magic casement, opening out onto a world which otherwise I could never have known',[7] and he was not alone in this view. Immediately after the First World War the availability of grants for ex-servicemen brought a huge influx of students, including many from New Zealand and Australia. Not all of them stayed the course, but among those who did were future Professors of Architecture at Auckland and Toronto and the future heads of architecture schools at Nottingham and Portsmouth.[8]

Women were always a small minority in the School. Reilly saw no reason why they should not succeed as architects, though he admitted that prejudice on the part of their male colleagues might tend to restrict them to a supporting role as assistants in larger practices.[9] Their record cards suggest a high proportion did not pursue architectural careers after graduation, but among those who did was Norah Dunphy (B.Arch. and Cert.Civic Design, 1926) who became Town Planning Assistant to Tynemouth and North Shields Corporation in 1931, the first woman to hold such a post.[10] Others, such as Frances T. Silcock (Dip.Arch. 1925), married student contemporaries and went into practice with them.

One of the most striking things about Reilly's School is the number of students it attracted from overseas, an average of five or six each year from 1919 to 1932, chiefly from countries then under British control such as Ceylon, Iraq, India and Egypt. Almost from the beginning, Reilly had aimed at an international reputation for the School through its publications. He sought to distribute its *Portfolio of Measured Drawings* in America,[11] and to arrange for sample copies of the *Liverpool Architectural Sketchbook* to be sent to Australia, Canada and Egypt[12]. The School prospectus, modelled on those of American schools of architecture and enticingly illustrated with prize-winning drawings by current students, also helped to spread the word overseas, and to William Holford (B.Arch. 1930), reading it in Johannesburg, it managed to convey 'the enthusiastic conviction that Liverpool was the architectural Mecca'.[13]

Outside England, Scotland and Wales the opportunities for an academic architectural training in the British Empire were limited: in 1920 the Liverpool School and the Architectural Association in London had become the first schools to have their five-year courses accepted in lieu of the final examinations for Associateship of the RIBA. The first colonial school to be thus exempted was McGill University, Montreal, in 1923, followed by a handful of schools in South Africa, Australia and New Zealand, but by 1937 there was still no school in Asia or the Middle East which offered exemption.[14]

Liverpool's position as an international port was another reason why students came to the city from overseas. According to J. S. Allen (B.Arch. 1922), a number of Reilly's South American students belonged to families linked to Liverpool by trade,[15] and similar connections may explain the occasional presence in the School of students from Norway, France, Holland, Spain, Belgium, the United States, and even Iceland. In some cases, the appointment of Reilly's graduates to positions of authority in foreign countries seems to have led to closer ties with the Liverpool School: Maurice Lyon (BA 1906) was Government Architect in the Ministry of Works in Cairo during the 1920s when a succession of Egyptian architecture students made the journey to Liverpool, and this pattern was repeated in Iraq where Harold C. Mason (Cert.Arch. 1911) was Government Architect at the same time.[16] The critic Frederic Towndrow did not exaggerate when he wrote of Reilly's achievement: 'It is difficult enough to create a school of architecture out of nothing; it was, indeed, Herculean to create an Empire centre of artistic culture in what is, in spite of its traditions, a provincial city'.[17]

One of the traditions Towndrow may have had in mind is the historic link between the port of Liverpool and the eastern seaboard of the United States. Reilly built on this link, his School became an important channel for the influence of contemporary American architecture in Britain, and his best students were given the chance to study American achievements at first hand through work placements in the offices of major New York architects.

Liverpool's transatlantic architectural connections date back at least to the first half of the nineteenth century, when the distinguished American neo-classicist William Strickland (1788–1854) visited the city and formed a lasting friendship with the dock engineer Jesse Hartley.[18] John Wellborn Root (1850–91) later spent two years of his schooling on Merseyside and it has been suggested that the example of Peter Ellis's pioneering Oriel Chambers in Water Street, then under construction, lies behind Root's innovative Chicago office buildings. In 1892 the brothers G. A. and W. J. Audsley, having made their names in Liverpool, emigrated to America and practised successfully in New York,[19] and the Liverpool Arts and Crafts designer H. Bloomfield Bare was active on both sides of the Atlantic.[20]

Reilly made his first visit to the United States in 1909, to investigate American town planning and visit schools of architecture there, and its effect on him was decisive. 'I am back from America with a new scale for life', he wrote to Reginald Blomfield on his return,[21] but it was not just the grandeur of American architecture which impressed him. In the classicism of architects like McKim, Mead and White and Carrère and Hastings—dignified, refined, eclectic yet scholarly, and free from excessive and vulgar ornament—he saw an architecture which, although rooted in the past, was essentially modern. It was the ideal corrective to what he considered the chaotic indiscipline of Edwardian architecture in Britain; and it was, moreover, a teachable style.[22] Reilly's reaction to America contrasts sharply with that of the Dutch architect H. P. Berlage who went there the following year and was chiefly impressed by the originality of Frank Lloyd Wright and Louis Sullivan, but it has much in common with the slightly later response of the German architectural writer Werner Hegemann.[23]

Reilly used his 1909 trip and subsequent visits to America to establish links with leading American architects. From them he acquired quantities of drawings and other materials to use as teaching aids,[24] the effects of which were soon apparent. A reviewer of the School's 1912 exhibition noted: 'It is, in fact, evident that the United States furnishes either the model or the inspiration for the composition, and even detail, of nearly every essay in design. But it is also clear that this enthusiasm for American achievement has behind it a sound knowledge of classic forms, and is not ill-considered or superficial in its nature . . . the manners of . . .

Charles Follen McKim, Hornbostle, Cass Gilbert and Van Buren Magonigle are the chief favourites'.[25] J. S. Allen (B. Arch. 1922), who taught at the School in the early 1930s, confirms that as students even men like Maxwell Fry and George Checkley, who later made their names as modernists, 'had no horizons beyond the drawings of McKim, Mead and White'.[26]

In 1909 one of Reilly's first students, Herbert J. Rowse (Cert. Arch. 1907), also made the journey from Liverpool to North America. He followed in the footsteps of Frank Simon (1863–1933), designer of the Liverpool Cotton Exchange, and worked for Simon on the Manitoba State Legislative Building. Later, many more of Reilly's best students were to have the chance of absorbing American architecture at its source thanks to their Professor's New York connections. In 1920, with the help of the New York architect Benjamin W. Morris, three Liverpool students spent their summer vacation working in architects' offices there,[27] and such placements continued annually until the Wall Street Crash of 1929. The work undertaken by these students varied considerably. William Holford found himself subjected to the tedium of correcting working drawings in the office of Voorhees, Gmelin and Walker but his friend Gordon Stephenson got the prestigious job of drawing out and rendering the presentation plan of Corbett, Harrison and MacMurray's first, unexecuted, design for Rockefeller Center.[28] Maxwell Fry was employed on one of Carrère and Hastings's Long Island mansions, though he supplemented his income with freelance perspective work, and George Kenyon worked for Shreve, Lamb and Harmon on the elevations of the Empire State Building.[29]

The relevance of these experiences to ordinary practice in Britain might seem doubtful, but in fact all the students named above were to work on projects of the greatest size and complexity in their future careers, from the construction of new universities to the laying out of new towns and cities. Big American offices offered a foretaste of the large architects' departments within municipal authorities and public bodies where many of Reilly's students would later work. John Henry Forshaw (B. Arch. 1922), who spent the Summer of 1920 with Flagg and Chambers in New York, went on to head the architectural department of the Miners' Welfare Committee and compared its division into project-based teams with the organisation of a large American office.[30] But whatever practical lessons Reilly's students may have learned in New York, these placements were above all a way of fuelling their ambition by putting them at the architectural centre of the world's most prosperous, confident and technologically advanced society.

On Merseyside, the years of Reilly's professorship saw a definite move away from opulent Edwardian classicism, typified by Briggs and Thornely's Mersey Docks and Harbour Board building of 1907, towards a more restrained classicism of the American kind. Reilly and his students played a significant part in this.

Among Reilly's graduates who pursued their careers in Liverpool the most

Fig. 11 (Cat. 81) Edward Chambré Hardman, 'Water Street, Liverpool, 1929', showing Martins Bank under construction. (The E. Chambré Hardman Trust)

Fig. 12 (Cat. 82) Edward Chambré Hardman, 'Water Street and Dale Street, Liverpool', 1932, showing Martins Bank completed. (The E. Chambré Hardman Trust)

important was Rowse. His India Buildings and head quarters for Martins Bank are among the outstanding commercial buildings of their date in the country, and are designed in direct emulation of contemporary American models. During these years his office became an important employer of Reilly-trained architects: it was due to Reilly that J. S. Allen returned from America to work as Rowse's assistant on India Buildings,[31] and he was followed by others such as Donald Bradshaw and George Kenyon (Dip. Arch. 1930) whose Liverpool School training meant they could be relied on for fine draughtsmanship and a sound knowledge of classical detail.

Outside Rowse's office, former students in private practice and public employment were also building on Merseyside in the 'Liverpool manner'—a term coined by the critic Randall Phillips to describe the School's particular brand of classicism.[32] Herbert Thearle (Dip. Arch. 1925) won the competition for the Williamson Art Gallery at Birkenhead in partnership with L. G. Hannaford; Leonard Barnish (Cert. Arch. 1903, Dip. Civic Design 1914) designed banks for Lloyds in Victoria Street and Bold Street; Frederick Hamer Crossley (Dip. Arch. 1925) did the Birkenhead Central Library; and H. H. Davies was responsible for numerous public houses which lend an air of classical refinement to their suburban

Fig. 13 The Blackburne Arms, Catharine Street, Liverpool, remodelled by Harold Hinchliffe Davies, c.1927, photograph by Edward Chambré Hardman (The E. Chambré Hardman Trust)

settings. H. W. Pritchard (Cert. Arch. 1921), after a spell in Lutyens's office working on New Delhi, returned to Liverpool and a job in the office of the city's Land Steward and Surveyor. He was responsible among other things for the classical car depot in Edge Lane and the grand park entrance in Harthill Road, constructed from fragments of a nineteenth-century Italianate office building by James Picton.[33] H. S. Silcock (B. Arch 1924) worked for the city from 1925 to 1928 and designed the dignified neo-Georgian Police and Fire Stations at Allerton, and the layout of the adjoining houses.[34]

It is fair to point out that many of the city's most prominent buildings in the 'Liverpool manner' were not designed by graduates of Reilly's School, though some may well be products of a climate of taste which Reilly helped to establish, through his lectures, journalism and personal contacts. Frank Simon's Cotton Exchange of 1905–06, which Reilly considered 'the best new building in the town',[35] was begun only a year after Reilly arrived on the scene and it anticipated many of the qualities he was to preach. The Adelphi Hotel, begun in 1912, was indebted to America in its refined classicism as well as its luxurious accommodation, but its designer, Frank Atkinson, had been an articled pupil of the Liverpool baroque architect J. F. Doyle and not a student at the School of

31

Architecture. In the field of commercial architecture, Gerald de Courcy Fraser (1873–1952) transformed Church Street, the city's main shopping area, with a number of big classical stores which won Reilly's approval by 'realising the value of simplicity and restraint, together with squareness of outline'; but Fraser had trained in the office of Walter Thomas, designer of exuberant Liverpool public houses such as The Vines and The Philharmonic.[36]

The buildings designed by Willink and Thicknesse from about 1910 onwards—for instance the School of Art and the Cunard Building—present a different case. In contrast to the firm's earlier work they show all the characteristics of the 'Liverpool manner', and may well reflect Reilly's direct influence: Reilly was Willink's neighbour at Dingle Bank, he seems to have shared Willink's office for a time,[37] and in 1914 his former student and associate Harold Dod (BA 1909) joined Willink and Thicknesse to work on the Cunard Building, later becoming a partner in the firm. A similar change can be seen in the output of Arnold Thornely's office at the same time, the baroque swagger of the Docks and Harbour Board offices giving way to the neoclassicism of the Geology building for Liverpool University, the extension and remodelling of the Walker Art Gallery, the West African Bank in Water Street, and the Northern Ireland Parliament Building at Stormont. A number of Reilly's students, among them the Rome scholars Herbert Thearle and F. O. Lawrence, worked for Thornely on Stormont.

As an occasional assessor of architectural competitions Reilly had both a platform for proclaiming his views and a chance to further the careers of his graduates. He awarded first prizes in the Liverpool and Dewsbury War Memorial competitions to men he had trained, and Herbert Rowse benefited twice from his judgements, winning the contests for Heswall Golf Club and—much more importantly—the new head office of Martins Bank. Working behind the scenes, Reilly was instrumental in obtaining the commission for St Gabriel's, Blackburn, for F. X. Velarde[38] (Dip.Arch. 1924), and he used his friendship with Spedan Lewis to get William Crabtree a job with the John Lewis Partnership, which resulted in Crabtree being commissioned to design the Peter Jones store in Sloane Square. For obvious reasons it is difficult to establish the extent of Reilly's patronage of his former students, but it would be surprising if these examples were exceptional. According to W. G. Holford (B.Arch. 1930) Reilly was a tireless promoter of his graduates: 'It was he who persuaded the heads of firms and the captains of industry, and even the selection committees of borough councils, to take on young architects who had very little practical training, but were full—he said—of imaginative ideas'.[39]

The greatest instance of Reilly's patronage might have been the appointment of one of his former students as Lutyens's successor to oversee the completion of Liverpool's Catholic Cathedral, but this was not to be. Reilly claimed that Archbishop Downey had promised to make such an appointment,[40] and when

Lutyens died in 1944 the Archbishop did indeed ask him to find a suitable 'continuator'.[41] Reilly wanted to put forward his prolific church-building graduate F. X. Velarde (Dip. Arch. 1924) for the job, but Velarde was unwilling and the appointment went instead to Adrian Gilbert Scott.[42]

Mention of Velarde, whose churches draw on Early Christian, Romanesque and Renaissance sources as well as contemporary church architecture in Germany, is a reminder that Reilly's students were not all homogeneous classicists. H. C. Bradshaw (Cert. Arch. 1913), winner of the first Rome Prize and one of the School's star graduates, worked at Burningfold Farm at Dunsfold, Surrey, in a thoroughgoing Old English style with leaded lights, tile hanging and half timbering.[43] On the other hand, H. G. Spencely (B. Arch. 1926) recalled preparing a design for a city gate with gothic towers, and discovering when he came to look for relevant illustrations in the School library that 'books on gothic were parcelled and kept on top of the library shelves, lest they contaminate us'.[44] The point which

Fig. 14 Francis Xavier Velarde, St. Monica's church, Bootle, photograph by Edward Chambré Hardman, c.1936 (The E. Chambré Hardman Trust)

Reilly insisted on repeatedly in his writings, namely the need to combat excessive individuality among architects,[45] seems an unlikely principle with which to excite enthusiasm among the young, eager and creative. But in practice Reilly's commitment to classicism does not appear to have been regarded by his students as a straitjacket. He positively encouraged originality and imagination,[46] not least through the six-hour sketch designs which the whole School produced each week, the aspect of Reilly's teaching most often recalled with pleasure by those who studied under him. Reilly's critical writings show that as well as purer forms of classicism he could enjoy the 'splendid make-believe' of Liverpool's Loire Chateau-style General Post Office and the Piranesian, cathedral-like machine shop of a local foundry.[47] He was, he recognised, torn between two conflicting tastes, for the orderly and rational on the one hand, and for 'a certain swagger and drama' on the other.[48] When, in the late 1920s and early 1930s, continental modernism in its various more or less austere forms finally overcame the 'Liverpool manner', Reilly still felt the attraction of a more romantic tradition of building and predicted its eventual revival: 'when we are tired of our cubes and rectangles', he wrote, 'we shall have another baroque reaction'.[49]

Beyond Merseyside, Reilly's graduates pursued successful careers both in private practice and as assistants in larger offices. The work of a representative selection is illustrated in *The Book of the Liverpool School of Architecture*, published as a tribute to Reilly at the time of his retirement, and further examples are listed in the catalogue of an exhibition of the work of past students held at the Royal Institute of British Architects in 1937.[50] These sources, however, give only a limited impression of the large number of Liverpool-trained architects who entered public service and, working more or less anonymously, rose to positions of influence in government departments, municipal authorities and other public bodies. In retirement, Reilly found so many of his former students applying for jobs in the public sector that he was often called on to provide references for several candidates on the same shortlist.[51] In the 1950s the city architects of Birmingham, Manchester, Newcastle upon Tyne and Southampton were all former students of Reilly's,[52] and the rebuilding of large parts of these cities was in their hands. The links between such post-war urban redevelopment and the taste for the 'Grand Manner' taught at Liverpool under Reilly and Patrick Abercrombie merit investigation.[53]

The Liverpool School has been seen as a pioneer in encouraging the idea that architects should strive to improve the daily lives of ordinary people[54]—a central belief of the Modern Movement—and it is true that the existence of the Department of Civic Design within the School made students think about the broader social and environmental setting of their work. But any wholehearted conversion of the School to 'social architecture', such as Walter Gropius described in 1936,[55] seems to have come right at the end of Reilly's professorship and to have developed further after his departure. Reilly's Roscoe Lecture, 'The Body of the Town', a strongly felt plea for architectural solutions to urban social problems, was delivered in 1934, the year after he left Liverpool.[56] Bruce Allsopp, a student during this period, felt that his contemporaries in the School were 'not much concerned with putting the world to rights', that they were not on the whole political, and that they still believed 'an architect's job was to produce beautiful buildings'.[57] Nevertheless, a significant number of the men Reilly had trained became prominent in fields such as social housing, with a strong commitment to architecture as a public service. J. H. Forshaw in his work for the Miners' Welfare Committee is perhaps the outstanding example. Another is Christian Barman (Cert. Arch. 1918), who through his work for the London Passenger Transport Board and as a freelance product designer for HMV put his talents at the service of the mass market.

When the Depression in the United States ruled out the traditional New York office placements, a large number of Reilly's students went for their office experience to the Housing Department of Liverpool Corporation where the Director of Housing, Lancelot Keay, was engaged in a major building programme;[58] some were employed by him after graduation. Gordon Stephenson planned the layout of the Dovecot estate on the outskirts of Liverpool,[59] and John

Fig. 15 Perspective drawing by Leonard Berger of John Hughes's design for St. Andrew's Gardens, Liverpool, 1934 (City of Liverpool Libraries and Information Services, Liverpool Record Office)

Hughes (B.Arch. 1931) and Leon Berger worked on the great complex of city centre flats called St Andrew's Gardens. Hughes went on to become Director of Housing in Manchester and, later, Westminster; Berger went to Salford Corporation as Assistant Architect, then to Southampton where he became City Architect. William Crabtree was one of many Liverpool graduates to be invovled in the design of New Towns and social housing after the 1939–45 war; others include Anthony Minoprio (B.Arch. 1925) and S. Colwyn Foulkes.

Throughout the Reilly period a steady flow of graduates went overseas where work in the colonies and dominions, whether in an official capacity or in private practice, could give an architect scope to design on the grand scale for which his Liverpool training had prepared him. Frederick Williamson's work on the University of the Witwatersrand and other projects in South Africa, and Maurice Lyon's Post and Telegraph Office in Cairo are perhaps the most striking examples of exported Liverpool classicism conveying an imperialist message. Others tried to respond to the traditional architecture of the countries where they worked. P.C. Harris (Cert.Arch. 1910) as Government Architect in Zanzibar in the 1920s adopted an Islamic style for his additions to the Sultan's palace and other public buildings,[60] and H. C. Mason (Cert.Arch. 1911) drew on Middle Eastern models for his St George's church in Baghdad, regarded by Freya Stark as one of only two good buildings erected by the British in Iraq[61]. A. C. Holliday (B.Arch. 1922) and R. P. S. Hubbard (B.Arch. 1932) successfully combined aspects of European modernism with indigenous traditions in their work in Palestine, and of Hubbard's later work in Malta Reilly wrote that his former student was 'possibly the best man we have . . . to design simple modern buildings yet in sympathy with the Baroque architecture for which Malta is famous.'[62]

In Iraq and Egypt the dominance of official architects who were British-born and Liverpool-trained seems to have ended with the return to England of H. C. Mason and Maurice Lyon in the 1930s. Government posts in these countries were subsequently held by architects who were native-born, though still trained at Liverpool: Ahmed Mukhtar—a modernist—became government architect in Baghdad in 1938 and Mohamed El Hakim worked for the Ministry of Endowments in Cairo from 1934 to 1949. In his later career Hakim undertook major public commissions such as the Luxor Museum of Antiquities and the Nubia Museum at Aswan.

Students who attended the Liverpool School from overseas absorbed a thoroughly European training and their work, as reproduced in various School publications, appears indistinguishable from that of their British-born colleagues.[63] Mohammed Makiya, who came to Liverpool from Iraq in 1936, recalls that he brought with him little knowledge of Middle Eastern architecture, so did not experience the degree of cultural dislocation which might have been expected. In the long run his Liverpool training, with its requirement to produce measured

Fig. 16 (Cat. 102) Maurice Lyon, Post and Telegraph Office, Cairo, under construction, c.1927. (University Archives, University of Liverpool)

Fig. 17 (Cat. 103) Sultan's Palace and Baraza (Durbar Hall), Zanzibar, extended and altered by Philip C. Harris between 1926 and 1932. (University Archives, University of Liverpool)

drawings of historic buildings, led him to a greater awareness of the traditional architecture of his own country, and when he returned to Iraq as a teacher he introduced measured drawing into the syllabus there to stimulate his students' interest in vernacular architecture.[64]

By 1935 Reilly could write, apparently without irony, how strange it was 'that with the variety of climates and races included in the Empire, so few buildings with local characteristics are put up . . . in China, India, Africa, and Australia one finds the recent banks and office buildings [are] mostly rather degenerate London buildings . . . By watering down local tradition everywhere [photography] has helped to spread throughout the world the same pseudo-classical dress'.[65] It would be difficult to imagine a more complete reversal of the position he had held just ten years earlier, when he wrote approvingly of American classicism as 'a new international architecture'[66] and promoted it through publishing photographs of his own students' work. In time, of course, the modernism which Reilly had come to espouse would prove even more effective than classicism at eradicating regional and national architectural traditions.

Reilly had visited India in 1927–28 in the company of Lutyens, and his autobiography gives a tantalising glimpse of the two travelling companions—the soon-to-be modernist and the architect of imperial New Delhi—discussing Le Corbusier together on the outward voyage.[67] Reilly sent back a series of articles about his Indian travels which were published in the *Manchester Guardian* and the *Liverpool Post*[68] and which give a vivid impression of his enthusiastic response to the novel sights and experiences of the East—an impression confirmed by Lutyens, who wrote to his wife: 'Reilly is like a child, wildly excited and jumpy, points and waves his arms, says "goo goo" to everything'.[69] This playful remark makes a significant point, for it is probably true to say that infectious enthusiasm and an appetite for the new and different were the qualities that most distinguished Reilly's teaching and his School. He was not a profound theoretical thinker or a consistently outstanding designer of buildings, but among his students he created an atmosphere in which architecture was always a source of excitement. More than any one creed of design, Reilly gave his students a belief in the fundamental importance of architecture and an unswerving confidence—perhaps sometimes over-confidence—in their abilities. His style as a teacher was well summarised by W. G. Holford in a posthumous tribute to his old professor:

Fig. 18 Reilly and students in fancy dress, c.1930 (University Archives, University of Liverpool)

Looking back on those early years after a lapse of twenty years, I can recognise the animating principles by which our steps were guided. 'Prof's' advice to us, even if it was not expressed in so many words, was more or less as follows: 'Architecture is the Mistress Art, and has the most social significance. What you are setting out to do is enormously important and exciting, and will carry you into all sorts of interesting and adventurous places. It is bread and circuses for you all the way and at one and the same time. You have chosen a fortunate and inspiring profession; and [this to each group of students in succession] you look like becoming the best Year I have ever had in the School!'[70]

For thirty years this advice of Reilly's proved irresistible, and it helped shape a generation of architects in Britain and overseas.

Notes

1 Percy Johnson-Marshall, quoted in A. Saint, *Towards a Social Architecture: the Role of School-Building in Post-War England*, 1987, p. 241.

2 These figures and the other statistics which follow are calculated from the student record cards of the School. These are currently held by the School of Architecture and Building Engineering but will soon be transferred to the University Archives. I am grateful to Kay Hoare, a volunteer in the Walker Art Gallery, for compiling data from these cards.

3 L. Esher, *A Broken Wave: The Rebuilding of England 1940–1980*, 1981, p. 19.

4 *Building*, July 1937, p. 310, quoted in D. Dean, *The Thirties: Recalling the English Architectural Scene*, 1983, p. 37.

5 See comments on A. Minoprio in C. H. Reilly, *Scaffolding in the Sky—A semi-architectural autobiography*, 1938, p. 235.

6 Information from Mr R. Colwyn Foulkes. For S. Colwyn Foulkes see E. Hubbard, *The Buildings of Wales: Clwyd*, 1986.

7 Letter from Foulkes to Paul Reilly, 18 October 1963.

8 Cyril Knight, Eric Ross Arthur, George Checkley and Arthur Cecil Townsend.

9 See C. H. Reilly, 'Architecture as a Career for Men and Women', in *Journal of Careers*, March 1931.

10 L. Budden ed. *The Book of the Liverpool School of Architecture*, 1932, p. 44; student record card.

11 Liverpool University Archives, Reilly letter book, D207/2/1, 23 April 1906.

12 Liverpool University Archives, Reilly letter book, D207/2/3, 7 October 1910 and 1 February 1911.

13 W. G. Holford, 'Sir Charles Reilly: An Appreciation', *The Listener*, 15 July 1948, pp. 93–94.

14 See C. R. Knight, 'Architectural Education in the British Empire', *Journal of the Royal Institute of British Architects*, 22 November 1937, pp. 61–75. The author, Professor of Architecture at Aukland University College, New Zealand, had trained at the Liverpool School (B. Arch. and Cert. Civic Design 1923, MA 1925).

15 Interview with J. S. Allen, 28 February 1995.

16 Dr Mohammed Makiya confirms the influence of H. C. Mason in attracting Iraqi

students to the Liverpool School (interview, 18 January 1996).

17 Unidentified press cutting, c.1933, in a scrapbook owned by Anthony Minoprio. Frederic Towndrow (1897–1977) worked for a time as assistant to Herbert J. Rowse in Liverpool. In 1947 he went to Sydney as founding Professor of Architecture at the University of New South Wales.

18 For Strickland see A. A. Gilchrist, *William Strickland, Architect and Engineer, 1788–1854*, 1950.

19 See *Dictionary of American Biography*, 1928, vol. 1, pp. 422–23.

20 See catalogue of 1895 Spring Exhibition, Walker Art Gallery, Liverpool, nos. 378, 436 and 481.

21 Liverpool University Archives, Reilly letter book, S 3205, 3 May 1909.

22 See, for example, *British Architect*, 18 February 1910, and *Builder*, 30 July 1920; C. H. Reilly, *Some Architectural Problems of Today*, 1924, pp. 83–99; C. H. Reilly, *Mckim, Mead and White*, 1924. For the 'modernity' of twentieth-century American classicism see David B. Brownlee, *Building the City Beautiful: the Benjamin Franklin Parkway and the Philadelphia Museum of Art*, catalogue of an exhibition at the Philadelphia Museum of Art, 1989, chapter 1.

23 For these and other European responses to American architecture at this date see Jean-Louis Cohen, *Scenes of the World to Come: European Architecture and the American Challenge 1893–1960*, 1995.

24 Liverpool University Archives, Reilly letter book, S 3205, 12 May and 15 June 1909.

25 *Builders' Journal*, 10 July 1912.

26 Interview with J. S. Allen, 28 February 1995.

27 *Liverpool Post*, 29 October 1920.

28 Gordon Stephenson, *On a Human Scale—A Life in City Design*, 1992, pp. 21–22.

29 For Fry see Maxwell Fry, *Autobiographical Sketches*, 1975, pp. 95–98; information on Kenyon from press cuttings, local studies

collection, Newcastle upon Tyne Central Library.

30 J. H. Forshaw, 'The Architectural Work of the Miners' Welfare Committee', *Journal of the Royal Institute of British Architects*, 7 March 1938, p. 426.

31 Interview with J. S. Allen, 28 February 1995.

32 Op. cit. in note 5, p. 121.

33 Student record card.

34 Student record card.

35 Liverpool University Archives, Reilly letter book, D 207/2/1, 18 February 1907.

36 C. H. Reilly, *Some Liverpool Streets and Buildings in 1921*, 1921, pp. 24–27.

37 Liverpool University Archives, Reilly letter book, D 207/2/1, 27 June 1904.

38 *Architects' Journal*, 11 January 1934, p. 66.

39 Loc. cit. in note 13.

40 Op. cit. in note 5, p. 233.

41 Letter from Reilly to Archbishop Downey, 15 November 1944, enclosed in Building Fund Executive Committee minutes, Liverpool Metropolitan Cathedral Archives. I am grateful to David Crellin for this reference.

42 F. X. Velarde's diary entry for 28 May 1945 describes these events and gives his reasons for not wanting the job: he was unwilling to give the major part of his life to executing another's design, the suitability of which he doubted; he thought that as a local man he would be at a disadvantage with the building committee; and he believed that to build a cathedral on such a scale and at such a cost in the provinces was 'in very bad taste'.

43 See C. A. Farey and A. T. Edwards, *Architectural Drawing, Perspective & Rendering*, 1931, plate IX.

44 H. G. Spencely, autobiographical notes, Walker Art Gallery.

45 See, for example, op. cit. in note 36, pp. 11–18.

46 According to Bruce Allsopp, interview, 15 June 1995.

47 Op. cit. in note 36, pp. 49–50 and 80–81.

48 C. H. Reilly, *Representative British Architects of the Present Day*, 1931, p. 106–09.

49 Ibid., p. 119.

50 An Exhibition of the Work of Past Students and Members of the Staff of the Liverpool School of Architecture, RIBA, London, 30 April–14 May 1937.

51 Testimonial written for A. G. Sheppard Fidler, 7 January 1947.

52 A. G. Sheppard Fidler, Leonard C. Howitt, George Kenyon and Leon Berger.

53 In his work at Birmingham A. G. Sheppard Fidler concentrated on quality of design rather than quantity of production, and he resigned from his post when the city fathers turned to stytem-built tower blocks; see M. Glendinning and S. Muthesius, *Tower Block – modern public housing in England, Scotland, Wales and Northern Ireland*, 1994, pp. 247–51.

54 Op. cit. in note 1, pp. 5–7.

55 'Architects in the Making', An Exhibition by the Liverpool School of Architecture of the University of Liverpool at the Building Centre, 158 New Bond Street, London W1, 30 March–11 April 1936, opening address by Professor Walter Gropius, typescript, RIBA library.

56 Reprinted in op. cit. in note 5, pp. 321–39.

57 Interview with Bruce Allsopp, 15 June 1995.

58 See F. Newberry, *Flats in Liverpool, 1919–1939*, B.Arch. thesis, Liverpool School of Architecture, 1981.

59 Op. cit. in note 28, p. 27.

60 Liverpool University Archives, photograph album, A 152.

61 See Khalid Sultani, 'Architecture in Iraq between the Two World Wars 1920–1940', *International Magazine of Arab Culture*, 2/3, 1982, pp. 92–105. Freya Stark, 'Built on Sand' in Baghdad Sketches, republished by The Marlboro Press, c.1992.

62 Quoted by Lord Kinross in a letter to *The Times*, 3 September 1965.

63 See illustrations of work by S.P. Mehta in T*he Liverpool Architectural Sketchbook*, 1911, p. 113; S. Subhung in *The Liverpool University Architectural Sketchbook*, 1920, pp. 61, 81, and 87–91; and M. Riad in *The Book of the Liverpool School of Architecture*, 1932, plates XXXI–XXXIV. Subhung had been educated in England—at Oundle—before coming to Liverpool. Bruce Allsopp recalls that one of his contemporaries, Tat Cho Yuen from Hong Kong (d. 1988), was exceptional for designing in a Chinese style.

64 Interview, 18 January 1996.

65 'Some More Empire Banks', *The Banker*, February 1935, p. 274.

66 Op. cit. in note 36, p. 10.

67 Op. cit. in note 5, p. 267. With Reilly's help, Lutyens wrote a review of *Towards a New Architecture* for *The Observer* (Lutyens's letters to his wife, RIBA Archives, 4 January 1928). The review is reprinted in Mary Lutyens, *Edwin Lutyens*, 1980, pp. 285–87.

68 See op. cit. in note 5, pp. 267–85.

69 RIBA Archives, Lutyens to his wife, 17 January 1928.

70 Loc. cit. in note 13.

C. H. Reilly
and the First Lord Leverhulme

MICHAEL SHIPPOBOTTOM

Great though Reilly's achievements were it is doubtful if they would have been so speedily and comprehensively attained without the help and encouragement of William Hesketh Lever, the first Lord Leverhulme (1851–1925). Certainly the Lever Prizes in the School of Architecture, the saving of the eighteenth-century Bluecoat School in Liverpool, new buildings for the School of Architecture, and in particular, the founding of the new department of Civic Design within the School, would have been unimaginable without Lever's support.

Early expansion of his father's grocery business in Bolton had led Lever and his brother to diversify into soap production, initially in Warrington, then from 1888 at a new factory across the Mersey from Liverpool on a 'green field' site at Port Sunlight with model housing alongside. Port Sunlight combined for the first time on any scale picturesque visual traditions with those of social improvement and better housing for industrial workers.[1]

Lever never tired of restating his wish to have been an architect, and with the massive expansion of the Lever Brothers firm and his own soaring personal wealth, he became one of the most important private building patrons of the twentieth-century, ultimately involved in the planning or re-planning of some ten towns and villages by the time of his death. In 1905 he first met Thomas Mawson (1861–1933), the leading British landscape architect who was to have a profound influence on Lever's estate and garden planning, and he enjoyed friendships with a number of architects, in particular Jonathan Simpson (1850–1937), his closest friend throughout life, and his son James Lomax-Simpson (1882–1977), together with the Owen family in Warrington. These friendships helped reinforce Lever's natural interests in architecture and planning.[2]

With firm convictions, unswerving faith in their own abilities, and with similar visionary and propagandist leanings, Reilly and Lever possessed many of the same raw qualities. It was perhaps inevitable that two such active men within a few miles of each other would cross paths sooner or later. Reilly determined it would be sooner,[3] and on the pretext of making arrangements for his students to visit Port Sunlight within his first term had gained admission to Lever himself. The description of their uneasy first meeting is one of the highlights in Reilly's autobiography.

Having left school directly to join his father's business, Lever had mixed views on the benefits of a university education: '. . . my own feeling is that Cambridge and Oxford Universities dull the edge of a man for business, but that they eminently suit him as an all-round sincere and capable man for public and social duties as well as business . . .'[4] Reilly's Queens' College background might therefore have counted against him in Lever's eyes, but perhaps because he was naturally not an academic they quickly seem to have established a rapport.[5] In time Lever was to be a generous donor to universities in Bristol, Edinburgh and Cheshunt College, Cambridge, as well as Liverpool University, and he even held out the prospect of a university to be established in his home town of Bolton.[6]

At Port Sunlight Lever encouraged an Arts and Crafts studio run by H. Bloomfield Bare, a Liverpool architect noted for his contribution to the decoration of the Philharmonic Hotel in Liverpool. In 1904 Bare organised an Arts and Crafts Exhibition in the Port Sunlight Gymnasium which was opened by Sir Martin Conway, at that time Slade Professor of Art but who had earlier held Reilly's Roscoe Chair in Liverpool.[7] Reilly and his wife were invited to the opening luncheon party. It was the beginning of a period of close contacts, with Reilly visiting Lever on alternate Sundays at Port Sunlight and joining Lever and his wife for lunch at Thornton Manor. In William Holford's words, it was a '. . . typical Renaissance arrangement, and suited Reilly down to the ground . . .'[8] Reilly was at liberty to suggest architectural schemes which would use up Lever's capital, provided that Lever was equally free to refuse.[9]

Reilly was immediately keen to involve Lever in the University, and early on a scheme was apparently discussed for moving the faculty of Arts to a new building in the Old Haymarket facing across St John's Gardens to St George's Hall. His dramatically inflated design for this was shown at the 1905 Royal Academy Exhibition,[10] but it could hardly have been considered a serious project, though in its use of the twin Greenwich Hospital domes it nicely anticipates his more mature London County Hall design of 1907.

His appointment to the School of Architecture, then a part of the 'City of Liverpool School of Architecture and Applied Art' within the University, had coincided with the transfer of the applied art section to the City's own School of Art.[11] Although dismissive of the value to architectural students of this decorative crafts-dominated section, Reilly had no doubts about the value of some of its former staff who had included Anning Bell, Augustus John and Herbert McNair.[12] A plan put forward by Reilly to Lever shortly after would have helped redress the situation by forming a completely new faculty of Fine Arts comprising, in addition to the existing School of Architecture, chairs in Aesthetics, Painting, Sculpture and Music. According to Reilly all this was to be funded by Lever who seemed '. . . genuinely keen . . . there was no doubt about his love of the arts and his desire to promote them . . .' The archive correspondence, however, makes clear that Lever was only prepared to establish one chair of Art, provided funds for other departments were obtained from other sources; but these were simply not forthcoming.[13] The Corporation had anticipated the possible future value of such a faculty in an Education Committee Report of 1904, but were alarmed at the prospect of immediate competition with their own newly expanded School of Art, and after a delegation visited Lever at Port Sunlight, the whole project was dropped.[14]

Despite Lever's withdrawal, the scene had been set for a more active involvement, and fruitful contacts next developed as a result of the continuing growth of Port Sunlight.

Cottages in the village were built in distinct phases, the product eventually of some twenty-four different architectural practices, but mostly dominated by the work of four firms and from 1910 by the work of James Lomax-Simpson, in effect the company architect. In 1905 there was a further burst of activity with new development concentrated around Pool Bank, Central Road and Lower Road. For this Lever seems to have deliberately encouraged contributions from architects previously not represented in the village, and a competition was held for at least some of the blocks: G. E. Deacon and Horsburgh were awarded first prize, and in a special category for architectural assistants the award was given to William Naseby Adams (c.1887–1952), then still a pupil of Reilly.[15] Adams was only eighteen at the time his block was built at 5–13 Central Road, a testimony to Lever's willingness to trust and to take risks. Despite Adams's sometimes unpredictable behaviour (Roderick Bisson recounts the story of him asking for his winnings for the Port Sunlight cottages to be paid in guineas which he then showered over himself) the trust seems to have been well placed: after a period in Liverpool practice Adams became chief assistant to Lutyens on Britannic House and sat on the Council and various committees of the RIBA.[16] A surviving unexecuted design by Herbert J. Rowse, another of Reilly's young protégés, also for cottages on Central Road and of this date, may have been submitted for the same competition.[17]

In 1906 Reilly himself contributed a block of cottages to Port Sunlight, but whereas most buildings in the village were influenced by the Old English manner of Shaw and Nesfield, Reilly's block is unusual for its almost Regency style—more suggestive of the later Portmeirion than Port Sunlight. W. L. George in the first major independent account of the village criticised the block for its verandah which he felt '. . . effectually excludes sunshine from the ground floor. This is the one and only instance of such a mistake . . .'[18] More importantly, Lever himself was dissatisfied and later considered demolishing the block as part of a replanning exercise for the Diamond.[19] But this did not deter Reilly, and though he did not refer to the block in his autobiography, he was later to ask Lever for information on the houses so that he could discuss their design with a

Fig. 19 (Cat. 62) Charles Reilly, cottages at 15–27 Lower Road, Port Sunlight (British Architectural Library, RIBA, London)

potential client.[20] The project was to remain Reilly's only major executed commission for Lever.

Lever's successful libel actions against the *Daily Mail* and other papers, enforcing the retraction of allegations that Lever Brothers had been involved in a monopolistic soap cartel, were amongst the great legal battles of the era. They provided Lever with damages ultimately totalling £91,000,[21] which though by rights due to the firm of Lever Brothers, were in fact used by Lever as sole ordinary shareholder. For Reilly, this windfall opened up mouth-watering possibilities which within a year were all being realised simultaneously, but of which the founding of the Department of Civic Design remains by far the most important and influential.

Initially Reilly had not been to the fore as the pressure for town planning control gathered momentum in the early years of this century, but he became increasingly involved in its grander visions and in projects of metropolitan scale, both in the design work of the School of Architecture and his own practice. Reilly was sure that the studies involved in the new subject of town planning should be undertaken in the context of architectural training and was determined that the right place for this was his own School. In 1907 he took an active part in the City Beautiful Conference held in Liverpool at which he denounced the 'surfeit of the picturesque'.[22] For Reilly there was no question that urban town planning should be in the Beaux Arts classical manner,[23] and he sympathised with Lever's view that town planning was but 'architecture on a big scale'.[24] Many years later he recalled driving up Whitehall with Lever and noticing that '. . . he had an eye for big monumental ideas in Architecture . . . he remarked with approval on the monumental dignity the range of raised columns gives to the War Office . . .'[25] Lever's town planning interests had developed over many years. He believed in town planning as an art, as a social necessity and as good business, but initially his involvement with the subject grew out of his concern for improved housing. It was this which had motivated the free flowing picturesque layout of the early part of Port Sunlight. But later additions to the plan exhibited a more formal character, particularly following Lever's enthusiastic visit to the then incomplete World's Columbian Exposition in Chicago in 1892,[26] the harbinger of the American City Beautiful movement.

If Reilly's interest in planning was timely, even a little opportunistic, Lever's pre-eminent position derived from the early development and continuing influence of Port Sunlight in the Garden City movement, and he played host or patron in many early twentieth-century key events and conferences. Both the two leading organisations campaigning for town planning legislation, the National Housing Reform Council and the Garden Cities Association, visited or held conferences at Port Sunlight, and Lever was active in the formation of the First Garden City at Letchworth, where he became a director, and at Hampstead Garden Suburb, where he was a trustee. In several key speeches—at Birkenhead in 1893,[27] at the Conference of Municipal authorities meeting in Sheffield in 1905[28] and at the 1906 Housing Conference in Sheffield—Lever advocated that councils should purchase cheap peripheral land and lay it out carefully for development by private developers.[29] The planning of new areas in an attempt to relieve overcrowding of city centres was a key feature of the 1909 Town Planning Act, but both Reilly and Lever, though welcoming the new legislation, realised its limitations in dealing with housing and suburban areas but not with existing centres nor, specifically, with architectural treatment.[30] Reilly and Lever shared a sense of the inferiority of Britain's grand architecture and planning in comparison with the achievements of her European neighbours and America. Reilly's sympathy with '. . . the reproach that had long rested on us in England that monumental architecture was beyond our scope . . .'[31] found an echo in Lever's own views on the parsimony and lack of vision shown in British public buildings and planning.[32]

The need for a recognised, appropriate, formal training in planning was clear. T. H. Mawson, a closer friend of Lever than Reilly and increasingly involved in town planning since his report on Pittencrief Park, Dunfermline in 1904,[33] had apparently come to this same view, but it was Reilly who was to get Lever interested by writing to him broaching the idea of a Department of Town Planning within the School of Architecture. According to Reilly, '. . . by return of post the matter was practically settled . . .',[34] and Lever generously acknowledged Reilly's action: '. . . I can only say that professor Reilly by his enthusiasm in the cause of

Town Planning has been the influence that has brought this matter to a definite stage earlier than would otherwise have been the case . . .'[35] This decision, according to Myles Wright, author of the definitive early history of the Department, was probably taken in May or June 1908.[36] Initially Lever offered £500 for foreign travel to collect material with a view to publishing a report, with a further £500 to £1,000 a year over three years for continued research and instruction[37] By early 1909 these proposals had been firmed up with Lever contributing £1,000 for three years to equip a separate Department within the School of Architecture, with a capital sum of £1,500 for research.[38]

For natural salesmen like Reilly and Lever the name of the new Department was important: '. . . I feel that the title of "Town Planning and Landscape Architecture" is cumbersome, and that we ought to get a better title. What I want, seeing that it is an entirely new idea, is that there shall be no misconception as to the field to be covered. I will think over the name you suggest, which has the great merit of shortness . . .', wrote Lever.[39] The title Reilly had suggested was Civic Design.

To head the new Department an architect friend of Reilly from his London days was appointed on Reilly's recommendation, Stanley Adshead (1868–1946), a notable perspective artist and fellow enthusiast for the 'mature classical architecture for which the Liverpool School stood'.[40] Lever took to him—particularly on finding he had 'grafted a metropolitan experience on to a north country stock'.[41] Within the new Department a number of specialists were quickly assembled including Patrick Abercrombie (1879–1957), appointed as research fellow,[42] and Lever's friend Thomas Mawson (1861–1933) for landscape design.

With the Department well under way to being established, Reilly and Lever found new acclaim and wasted few opportunities to promote the cause of town planning and with it the Department's success. They were, for instance, both in attendance at H. V. Lanchester's important talk on town planning at the RIBA in February 1909, at which Lever spoke in the discussion and Reilly proposed a vote of thanks mentioning the 'serious responsibility' now placed on him in starting up this first school of town planning.[43] Both attended the RIBA Annual Dinner in London with Lever again making an address. In August both took part in a National Town Planning Congress held by the National Housing Reform Council in Liverpool and Port Sunlight, joined in this by Mawson, Adshead and also by Professor Berlepsch Valendas of Munich—a notable German architect and writer who published a detailed and enthusiastic account of Port Sunlight.[44] The 1910 Congress of the Royal Institute of Public Health was held in Birkenhead under the presidency of Lever and featured a town planning section in which both Reilly and Adshead delivered papers.[45] But crowning all their efforts was the RIBA Town Planning Conference and Exhibition of 1910. It was by far the grandest of these conferences, with a major exhibition mounted at the Royal Academy and with the King as Patron. Myles Wright notes how with four Liverpool men giving papers

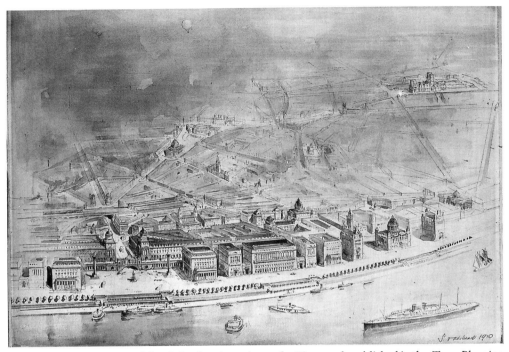

Fig. 20 (Cat. 90) Stanley Adshead, Replanning scheme for Liverpool, published in the *Town Planning Review*, July 1910 (The Board of Trustees of the National Museums & Galleries on Merseyside: Walker Art Gallery)

including Reilly himself, and with even the Conference banquet menu card having been designed by Liverpool students, Reilly must have felt a fully-earned satisfaction.[46] Lever attended the inaugural meeting and banquet, and Port Sunlight was well represented in the exhibition with drawings included in both the Garden Cities section and Mawson's own display. Reilly's membership of the RIBA Town Planning Committee from 1910 and the award of Honorary Associateship of the RIBA to Lever in the same year, show the profession's recognition of their respective efforts.

Lever's funding of the Department was specifically intended to cover travel in connection with research, allowing Reilly to visit America's eastern seaboard to investigate the curricula of American institutions and schools as well as to observe town planning methods in practice, and Adshead to visit Europe.[47] Their findings helped to shape the infant Department and found their way into the stream of articles which began to fill the *Town Planning Review*.

No strangers to the power of publicity and the press, for Reilly and Lever the production of the *Town Planning Review* from 1910 as the public organ of the new Department was an integral part of it. In 1906 Reilly had published his students measured drawings and from 1910 onwards four volumes of the *Liverpool Architectural Sketch Book* appeared. Lever had begun producing a house magazine as early as 1885 in the form of *The Lancashire Grocer* followed later by *Progress* and various Sunlight year books and almanacs. He had conceived the lavish *History of Rivington* to coincide with the opening of Lever Park on his Rivington estate in 1904, and later with the opening of the Lady Lever Art Gallery he was to initiate the impressive triple volume catalogue of the collection.

The *Town Planning Review* had a serious purpose and quickly established itself as the principal journal in the field, publishing the work of the Department and illustrating examples from abroad as well as home. The journal's first editor was Patrick Abercrombie who noted that the *Review*, though published on the urging of Reilly, was Lever's 'especial creation, and in its difficult initial years was kept alive by his encouragement and support'.[48] Not surprisingly it illustrated or recorded many of Lever's own projects such as the 1910 replanning scheme for Port Sunlight; the Wirral Avenues; the replanning scheme for Bolton; and Lever Park, Rivington. It particularly encouraged debate on Lever's offer of the Storeton Estate to Birkenhead in line with his often advocated view that councils should purchase land on their outskirts for development, particularly apposite following the 1909 Act, and it published invited views on this, including contributions from J. S. Nettlefold and Raymond Unwin. Adshead even prepared some preliminary proposals for Birkenhead but the sale was stopped and by the 1920s Lever was actively considering his own building schemes for the area.[49] Whether or not Lever distributed copies of the *Review* among 'members of Parliament and other prominent people' as urged by Reilly,[50] by the second year of publication its circulation had reached a thousand copies—with large numbers going to America and Germany.[51]

In 1914 Adshead left Liverpool to take up an appointment as professor in the newly created Department of Town Planning at University College, London, established as a direct consequence of the Liverpool School. Lever gave this his support. He presided at Adshead's inaugural address[52] and from 1915 onwards contributed annual prizes. However, Adshead's suggestion that production of the *Town Planning Review* might be shared between the two schools was, not surprisingly, quickly squashed by Reilly who felt it was too valuable an organ of the Liverpool School.[53] With Lever's support Abercrombie was appointed Adshead's successor in Liverpool for 1915–36 before he followed Adshead southwards, to become perhaps Britain's best known town planner. Given the extraordinary growth of town planning as a discipline since 1909, with the establishment of over 120 courses by 1981[54] and with the profession as secure and established as any, the importance of Reilly persuading Lever to make a comparatively small contribution to Liverpool University in 1908 cannot be over-estimated.

Fig. 21 (Cat. 14) 'Liberty Buildings', the former Bluecoat School, Liverpool. Drawing by Stanley Adshead and Harold Chalton Bradshaw, reproduced in the Prospectus of the School of Architecture for the Session 1910–11 (University Archives, University of Liverpool)

Now known as the Bluecoat Chambers, the former Liverpool Bluecoat School, completed in 1718, is the oldest building in the city centre.[55] In 1906 the school moved to the suburbs and with the building's future in doubt, it was temporarily occupied by a group of artists. Faced with the threat of its redevelopment,[56] Reilly and Lascelles Abercrombie, Patrick Abercrombie's brother, prepared a public appeal which envisaged using the building as a centre for the arts as well as a home for the School of Architecture,[57] then housed in cramped attics in the University's Victoria Building. But the sale price was high and Reilly felt that 'the one hope was Lord Leverhulme'.[58] Not surprisingly Lever quickly became enthusiastic, for the Bluecoat was to be but one of a number of historic buildings in which he took an active interest, making possible their conversion to other uses. His saving of Hall I'th Wood, Bolton and conversion of it into a museum in 1899–1902, and his conversion of the medieval barns on his Rivington estate into public tea and function rooms in 1904, were to be followed by his transformation of Rivington Hall into a public art gallery in 1912; his purchase of Stafford House, partly for use by the London Museum, in 1912; and his later acquisition of Moor Park, Hertfordshire, for use as a country club in 1919.

According to Reilly it took the astonishingly short time of one week to make all the arrangements for the acquisition. Initially, Lever took a five-year lease on the building in 1909, granting the School of Architecture use rent-free alongside the already established artists, and offering to present the building to the University at the end of the five-year term or to provide funding for a completely new building instead.[59] The arrangement was designed by Lever to allow the University time to consider fully whether the building suited their purposes, particularly in view of its being sited well away from the main University core. In recognition of Lever's victory in his libel actions—the source of his funding—the building was renamed

Liberty Buildings (a name probably suggested by Reilly) and on Lever's wishes the name appeared as part of an inscription on the frieze of the main facade.[60] Reilly was empowered by Lever to undertake £1,200 worth of repairs and to design a small pedestal to house an album recording the successful libel actions.[61] The School moved into its new home in October 1909 after some adjustment of the artists' accommodation to allow the School full use of the first floor, giving Reilly an office facing across the entrance court to Adshead's immediately opposite.[62] The former chapel became the main studio. Reilly enthused about the space the building offered and both Reginald Blomfield and Aston Webb commented favourably on its facilities. Lever hosted a house warming later when the building looked resplendent in its new paintwork, and the RIBA Journal's correspondent underlined the high quality of students' work.[63]

But the School was to remain at the Bluecoat for only nine years, for the University decided in principle to take Lever's offer of finance for a new building

Fig. 22 (Cat. 15) Reilly and students in the main studio at Liberty Buildings, 1910 (University Archives, University of Liverpool)

even though Reilly felt on balance there were advantages to staying put.[64] The design of the new School was, however, entrusted by the University Council to Reilly and Adshead, perhaps in response to Reilly's earlier blasts at the University for overlooking him when selecting designs for other new University buildings, and a complaint to Lever in 1912 that because of his professorship 'large numbers of people imagine I am not in practice'.[65] In the event Adshead tactfully withdrew and the design was undertaken by Reilly and developed in 1914 into full working drawings. The site was on Bedford Street, close to the main University buildings and Reilly's then recently completed Students Union Building. The Beaux Arts style of Reilly's design owed much to America, and he openly praised McKim, Mead and White's comparable School of Architecture building at Harvard (1899–1902) as being the only appropriate building of its kind and 'typical of all that's best at the present moment in American architecture for which in a sense it stands'.[66] An elegant perspective was prepared by H. C. Bradshaw, one of Reilly's star pupils, and exhibited in the 1915 Royal Academy Exhibition where it drew favourable comment.[67] For Lever, whose idea it had been according to Reilly,[68]

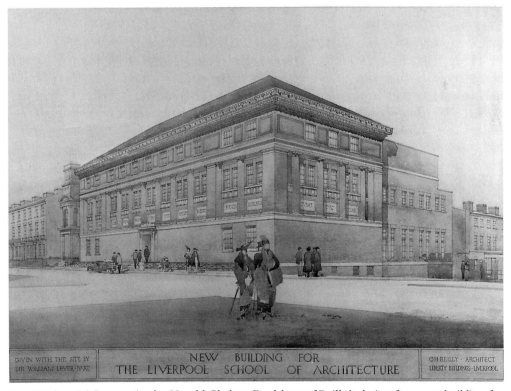

Fig. 23 (Cat. 74) Perspective by Harold Chalton Bradshaw of Reilly's design for a new building for the Liverpool School of Architecture, 1914 (University of Liverpool Art Gallery and Collections)

the design was very pleasing.[69] It must have made an instructive contrast with his other great commission then under construction, the Lady Lever Art Gallery in Port Sunlight, which had been designed by his architects W. & S. Owen also in a full blown Beaux Arts manner, after Lever had show them a photograph of a comparable American building.[70]

Reilly had discussed the Gallery with Lever in connection with student design subjects and though it had been agreed not to make a gallery the subject of the annual Lever prize, art gallery designs as well as designs for university buildings featured heavily in the 1913 *Liverpool Architectural Sketch Book* illustrating recent student work. It is ironic that the Lady Lever Art Gallery, perhaps the most complete expression of Reilly's ideals executed on Merseyside, should not have been designed by an architect from the Liverpool School, though in its disciplined, scholarly design it is clear from where some of its inspiration came.

The outbreak of war in 1914 saw work on the Lady Lever Art Gallery commenced on site, but the new School buildings sadly remained on paper only. It was during the war that gradual misunderstandings between Lever and the University came to a head over pension arrangements for Sir Ronald Ross at the School of Tropical Medicine, which had also been a recipient of Lever funding.[71] This disagreement, which Reilly felt the University had handled badly, soured relations with Lever, precipitating the move out of the Bluecoat, and the links were never satisfactorily reforged. The war may also have seen Lever reflecting further on the questionable benefits of a university education when he noted in 1917, the year of the rift, that there was 'a greater demand for craftsmen than for University men . . . We owe more to the craftsman than to the mere scholar or bookworm'.[72] Thus Lever failed to increase funding for the School when it was clear at the end of the war that his original offer of £24,000 would be insufficient for the new building. Only after Lever's death was new accommodation finally built in 1932–33, partly with additional funds contributed by the second Viscount Leverhulme. Designed by Reilly, Budden and Marshall, it forms a modern extension to the rear of a converted Georgian terrace in Abercromby Square, where Reilly had long advocated University expansion.[73]

The Bluecoat School building meanwhile had become the focus for proposals for a centre of the arts, in which Reilly and Lever again played leading roles. Coinciding with Lever's own plans across the Mersey to establish a major gallery, Reilly pleaded with him that the Bluecoat would offer a unique opportunity to provide a centre where artists could work alongside a '. . . small collection of the best work of past masters in pictures, sculpture and furniture . . .' and that if founded by Lever it would '. . . make Liverpool an art centre like Munich or even Paris, to give your collection a new lease of life. Too often art galleries were museums for dead things . . .'[74] Lever took the bait, though even he must have felt there was some little exaggeration here. A committee representing the occupants of the building, including Reilly, persuaded Lever to purchase it, and a scheme was drawn up by E. L. Bower for reconstruction.[75] This was given luke warm support by Reilly who may have felt that it was likely to be too prestigious a commission to fall into lesser hands, for shortly afterwards in March 1914 he left the committee and pursued the support of the centre with Lever independently,[76] though protesting that '. . . I have no desire to be employed in this matter professionally. I am too interested in the success of the idea . . .'[77]

Not surprisingly, Reilly's actions were viewed suspiciously by the Bluecoat committee, though Lever's decision that a scheme for the building should go to competition must finally have capped any ambitions Reilly may have held in that direction. The problem remained what sort of institution was to be founded in the building,[78] and though a draft Trust deed was drawn up in 1914 for this, the 'Lancashire Society of Arts', and approved by Lever, it remained in abeyance and the war intervened.[79] Perhaps it was his growing disenchantment with the University that in the end killed the project, or as Edward Morris has suggested, perhaps Lever, with his increasing interests in London, realised that such a scheme needed a metropolitan setting.[80] A revival of interest after the war was similarly doomed and by the time of Lever's death in 1925 the Bluecoat, though remaining in his ownership, had still not found a role.[81]

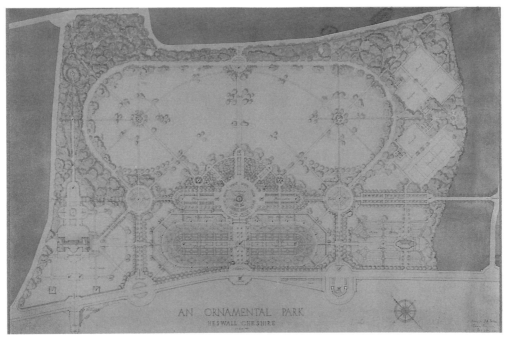

Fig. 24 (Cat. 95) John Henry Forshaw, An Ornamental Park, Heswall, Cheshire. This design won a Lever Prize in 1924 (Courtesy of Daniel Forshaw)

But Lever continued his involvement with the School of Architecture, largely in the form of annual prizes. He had begun by offering three prizes in 1909, of £20, £10 and £5, to be competed for by senior degree and diploma students in the School of Architecture and Department of Civic Design for re-designing the then incomplete central area of Port Sunlight. An additional fee of £100 was to be given if the scheme was implemented. The winner was Ernest Prestwich of the School of Architecture, whose design, as modified and extended by James Lomax-Simpson and T. H. Mawson, imposed on Port Sunlight a grandly formal axial plan.[82] Many years later Prestwich recalled how he felt like a 'millionaire' when he won and how he was discovered at Aintree racecourse by Reilly, who told him he shouldn't be wasting his money.[83]

Like the *Town Planning Review* the prizes afforded Reilly ample opportunity for publicity with regular reports in the architectural press as well as in the *Review* itself. For Lever also the prizes were not entirely altruistic. The first two subjects, Port Sunlight Central Area and a Block of Cottages, were intended for possible implementation, and even the 1912 prize subject, University Buildings on Brownlow Hill, may not have been just an academic exercise. Lever also had his architect Lomax-Simpson produce some ideas for the area[84] and Reilly noted to the Vice Chancellor that '. . . it would be a wonderful but not a quite impossible thing if Sir William took up seriously a scheme for this land . . .'[85] In 1911 the prize value was increased to a total of £50 in the form of two competitions, one for each department. The subject in the Department of Civic Design was a town planning scheme with a report on a particular Liverpool area, the competition being held in the autumn term, while in the School of Architecture, in the Lent term, the prize was for an architectural scheme for the same area.[86] The funding was arranged by Lever as required rather than as an endowment, which prompted Lever's obituary writer in the *Architects' Journal* (could this have been Reilly?) to enquire hopefully if it might continue after his death—sadly to no avail.[87]

The School and Reilly's own tastes clearly influenced Lever, and not just by way of the prizes. The promotion, for example, of the neo-Georgian mansion by the Liverpool School as the most appropriate model for post-war housing, coupled with consideration of industrialised building methods, was taken up in Lever's own speeches advocating standardisation and the use of concrete, and its influence may be seen in the later houses erected by him at Leverburgh on the Scottish island of Lewis, and not least in the hints of classicism creeping into Port Sunlight cottage design from 1919 onwards.[88]

In 1923 Lever was the guest invited to open the annual exhibition of student drawings, perhaps his last public contact with the School.[89] A review makes special mention of the 'brilliant' student Maxwell Fry—a reminder of the surprising new direction in which architecture was shortly to move. Lever's own tastes were changing too—as witness the black decorative schemes at the Lady

Lever Art Gallery in the 1920s or the late classical extensions by Mansfield at The Hill—but he certainly did not share Reilly's interest in the international Modern Movement. Reilly wrote in 1931 about his difficulty in understanding the 'museum point of view' which resulted in the decoration of rooms in every known style, and he must have found it increasingly difficult to accept Lever's love of just this approach to his own interiors; but then the two were a generation apart.[90] Already in 1922 Reilly had noted despairingly '. . . I wish I felt I could do anything personally with Lord Leverhulme in these days. He is so deaf that one cannot talk . . .'[91] A far cry from the days in 1909 when Lever, ever the businessman, ended a letter to the Vice Chancellor '. . . Always at your service . . .'[92]

Undoubtedly the Department of Civic Design remains the greatest memorial to the Reilly/Lever relationship and its importance was fully appreciated at the time. Yet Lever was curiously ambivalent about the new Department's abilities, perhaps because of his deteriorating relations with the University. While it is true he came to its rescue in 1915 he seems to have ignored the talents of Reilly, Adshead and Abercrombe in his own planning work, continuing to design layouts himself as in the case of the Bromborough Port Estate in 1910 and his villages in the Congo from 1913, or relying on T. H. Mawson and Lomax–Simpson for advice. Mawson admittedly is described as 'Lecturer in Landscape Design at the University of Liverpool' in the splendidly lavish proposals financed by Lever for replanning Bolton on monumental lines in 1910,[93] but the handsome perspectives were by Robert Atkinson rather than Adshead, and Reilly was not involved. Similarly, later reports on the agricultural and landscape potential of the island of Lewis and Harris and designs for Moor Park were both by Mawson, and Lever's support for improvements to Charing Cross Railway Bridge in 1916 makes no reference to Adshead's earlier ideas on the subject.[94]

Lever's death in 1925 prompted obituaries from both Reilly and Abercrombie, and references to Lever's vital support and his friendship surfaced in the tributes paid at the opening of Unilever House in 1932 and the new School building in 1933. Unilever House, where Lomax-Simpson had asked Reilly's advice on the appointment of executive architects, was reviewed by Reilly, who said he was convinced Lever would have been pleased with it. Reilly's awareness of Lever's enthusiasms and tastes had helped ensure his timely intervention in favoured projects and if their relationship had been strained and one-sided at times, the ultimate high standing achieved by both the School of Architecture and the Department of Civic Design is sufficient testimony to the very special and successful relationship which developed between these two dynamic and very similar personalities.

Acknowledgements

I am particularly grateful to the late Edward Hubbard for his great help on all Lever matters and for the use of his notes in the preparation of this essay; also to Adrian Allan, the University of Liverpool's Archivist; Edward Morris and Joseph Sharples of the National Museums & Galleries on Merseyside; John Tarn and John Hardie of the School of Architecture; Myles Wright; Dr Helen Power of the Liverpool School of Tropical Medicine; Victoria Lane of University College; the staff at the Heritage Centre, Port Sunlight; Robert Elwall and staff at the British Architectural Library, RIBA; and Maureen Staniforth at Unilever House.

Notes

1 For Port Sunlight see W. H. Lever, *The Buildings Erected at Port Sunlight and Thornton Hough*, 1902; Raffles Davison, *Port Sunlight*, 1916; W. L. George, *Labour and Housing at Port Sunlight*, 1909; E. Hubbard and M. Shippobottom, *A Guide to Port Sunlight Village*, 1988. For Lever see *Viscount Leverhulme*, by his son, 1927; W. P. Jolly, *Lord Leverhulme*, 1976.

2 For Lever's architectural interests see: Royal Academy Catalogue of the *Lord Leverhulme* exhibition, 1980; *Journal of the History of Collections* Vol. 4, 1992; M. Shippobottom, *Viscount Leverhulme: A Study of An Architectural Patron and his Work*, MA thesis, School of Architecture, Manchester University 1977.

3 Edward Hubbard's description of their first meeting.

4 Unilever House Archives, ref. TT3740, 157F, letter from Lever to his son, 13 January 1923, quoted in *Viscount Leverhulme*, pp. 224–45; W. P. Jolly, op. cit., p. 81.

5 T. Kelly, *For Advancement of Learning: The University of Liverpool 1881–1981*, 1981, p. 145; Myles Wright, *Lord Leverhulme's Unknown Venture*, 1982, p. 50; L. B. Budden, 'An Appreciation of Charles Reilly' in *Journal of the Royal Institute of British Architects* Vol. LV, 1948, pp. 212–13.

6 *Viscount Leverhulme*, pp. 254, 256–57.

7 *The Art Workers Quarterly* Vol. 3, 1904, p. 143; *Progress* Vol. 4, 1903, pp. 391, 469; Vol. 5, 1904, p. 235. The studio was at 14 Windy Bank, Port Sunlight c.1904–06.

8 W. G. Holford, 'Appreciation of C.H. Reilly' in *The Listener,* 15 July 1948, pp. 93–94.

9 C.H. Reilly, *Scaffolding in the Sky*, 1938, p. 123.

10 Reilly, op. cit., p. 123–24; *The Builder's Journal and Architectural Record*, Vol. 22, 1905, p. 225.

11 Reilly, op. cit., p. 85. There was an overlap of one session only.

12 Walker Art Gallery, *The Art Sheds, 1894–1905*, Exhibition Catalogue, 1981.

13 University of Liverpool Archives, correspondence of 1905–1906 between Reilly, Lever and the Vice Chancellor, A. W. W. Dale, first noted to the writer by Edward Hubbard; reference 5/12. See also Edward Morris in Royal Academy, op. cit., pp. 26–27.

14 Reilly, op. cit., pp. 124–25. According to Reilly, Lever was almost persuaded again after the First World War in connection this time with the Bluecoat School. Thomas Kelly, op. cit., p. 146. Kelly noted that some of Reilly's colleagues including the Vice Chancellor were also unhappy about the proposal. I am indebted to Edward Morris for sight of the City of Liverpool, *Education Committee Report on Secondary Education in Liverpool*, 1904, by M. E. Sadler.

15 *The British Architect*, Vol. 64, 1905, p. 478; *The Architects Journal, Vol.* 61, 1925, p. 728.

16 For Adams, see for example RIBA Biographical File; *Liverpool Daily Post*, 4 July 1952, appreciation by Lionel Budden; *The Builder*, Vol. 181, 1952, pp. 134–45, 169; R. F. Bisson, *The Sandon Studios Society and the Arts*, 1965, pp. 48, 67, 77; C. H. Reilly, op. cit., p. 236; C. H. Reilly, *Representative British Architects of the Present Day*, 1931, p. 79.

17 I am indebted to Joseph Sharples for discovering this. The drawing is dated 20 December 1905. A design by F. M. J. Owen published in *The British Architect*, Vol. 67, 1907, opp. p. 148 may also have been submitted in this same competition.

18 W. L. George, *Labour and Housing at Port Sunlight* 1909, p. 69. Lever's son noted that the group was interesting 'although hardly in keeping with the rest of the village'. See *Viscount Leverhulme*, p. 88.

19 According to James Lomax-Simpson in conversation with the writer, 21 August 1970.

20 University of Liverpool Archives, C. H. Reilly letters, D207/2/2, Reilly to Lever, 26 February 1906. The group is illustrated in T. Raffles Davison, *Port Sunlight*, 1916, p. 14, Fig. 18.

21 *Viscount Leverhulme*, pp. 138–39; W. P. Jolly, op. cit., pp. 46–55; C. Wilson, *The History of Unilever*, 1954, Vol. 1, pp. 83–88.

22 *Liverpool Daily Post and Mercury*, 28 and 30 June 1907; *The Builder* Vol. 83, 1907, pp. 1–2, 11–12.

23 *The Builder*, Vol. 88, 1905, p. 514; *Journal of the Royal Institute of British Architects*, Vol. 55, 1948, pp. 212–13. Appreciation of Reilly by Professor L. B. Budden refers to Reilly's long interest in town planning.

24 *Journal of the Royal Institute of British Architects*, Vol. 32, 1925, p. 460. Obituary to Lord Leverhulme by C. H. Reilly. See also Reilly, op. cit. in note 9, p. 126.

25 *Progress*, Vol. 32, 1932, p. 83.

26 See W. H. Lever, *Following The Flag*, 1893, p. 7.

27 W. H. Lever, 'Land for Houses' paper delivered to the North End Liberal Club, Birkenhead, 4 October 1898 in W. H. Lever, *The Six Hour Day*, 1918, p. 155.

28 *Progress*, Vol. 6,, 1905, pp. 412–24; Report of the Proceedings 1905; Rupert Hebblethwaite, 'The Municipal Housing Programme in Sheffield before 1914', *Architectural History*, Vol. 30, 1987, pp. 143–61.

29 *The British Architect*, Vol. 65, 1906, p. 391.

30 See for example letter from Lever in its support in *Garden Cities and Town Planning*, Vol. 3, 1908, p. 47; C. H. Reilly, op. cit. in note 9, p. 125.

31 *Journal of the Royal Institute of British Architects*, Vol. 16, 1909, p. 280.

32 See, for example, Lever, *Following the Flag*, 1893, pp. 104–05 and *Viscount Leverhulme*, p. 169.

33 T. H. Mawson, *The Life and Work of an English Landscape Architect*, 1927, pp. 100–01.

34 Loc. cit. in note 24 above.

35 Liverpool University Archives, 4/1/26, letter from W. H. Lever to Vice Chancellor A. W. Dale, 25 November 1908, also quoted in Martin Hawtree , 'The emergence of the Town Planning Profession' in A. Sutcliffe (ed.), *British Town Planning: The Formative Years*, 1981, pp. 94–95.

36 Wright, op. cit., p. 40.

37 *Journal of the Royal Institute of British Architects*, Vol. XVI, 1908, p. 143.

38 *The Builder*, Vol. 96, 1909, p. 383; *Journal of the Royal Institute of British Architects*, Vol. 17, 1910, p. 426.

39 Liverpool University Archives 4/1/26. Letter from Lever to Reilly, 20 November 1908. Budden refers to Reilly as a master of the art of publicity in his appreciation, in the *Journal of the Royal Institute of British Architects*.

40 Reilly, op. cit., p. 127; *The British Architect*, Vol. 71, 1909, p. 236. For Adshead, see C. H. Reilly, *Representative British Architects of the*

Present Day, 1931, pp. 152–7; Alan Powers, 'Architects I have known: The Architectural Career of S. D. Adshead', *Architectural History,* Vol. 84, 1981, pp. 103–23.

41 Patrick Abercrombie, Lever obituary in *Journal of the Town Planning Institute,* Vol. 2, 1924–25, p. 210; also Reilly, op. cit., in note 9, p. 127.

42 For Abercrombie, see especially Gerald Dix, 'Patrick Abercrombie 1879–1957', in G. E. Cherry, ed. *Pioneers in British Planning,* 1981.

43 *Journal of the Royal Institute of British Architects,* Vol. 16, 1909, p. 280.

44 H. E. Berlepsch Valendas, *Bauerhaus und Arbeiter Wohnung in England,* undated; information from Edward Morris; see also Alan Crawford, *C. R. Ashbee: Architect, Designer and Romantic Socialist,* 1985, p. 138 for visit of Valendas to Ashbee.

45 *Town Planning Review,* Vol. 1, 1910, pp. 261–62; *Viscount Leverhulme,* p. 257.

46 RIBA, *Transactions of the Town Planning Conference,* 1910; *Journal of the Royal Institute of British Architects,* Vol. 17, 1910, pp. 786–87; Wright, op. cit., pp. 57–58.

47 Reilly, op. cit. in note 9, pp. 123, 127–28; *Viscount Leverhulme,* p. 256; Liverpool University Archives, Annual Report of the Vice Chancellor, November 1909.

48 See Bisson, *op. cit.,* p. 52; obituary to Lever by Patrick Abercrombie.

49 *Town Planning Review,* Vol. 3, 1912, pp. 223–24, Vol. 4, 1913, pp. 13–25,

58 *Progress,* Vol. 22, 1922, pp. 192–93; *Viscount Leverhulme,* p. 298. Letter from S. D. Adshead to J. Fearnley, Borough Engineer, 27 January 1913 in the Lady Lever Art Gallery archives. I am grateful to Edward Morris for drawing my attention to this last.

50 Liverpool University Archives, S3206, letter from Reilly to Lever, 8 August 1910.

51 Liverpool University Archives, report by Reilly to Senate, 20 March 1912.

52 *The Builder,* Vol. 107, 1914, p. 447–48; *Journal of the Town Planning Institute,* February

1939, pp. 126–27; *The British Architect,* Vol. 82, 1914, pp. 207, 231–40; Wright, op. cit., p. 28; Annual Report UCL, 1915, p. 33; Minutes of the College Committee, 12 January 1915; letter from Adshead to Professor Butler, University College, 12 October 1925. I am grateful to Victoria Lane of University College library for these references.

53 University of Liverpool archives, S3212, letter from Reilly to Lever, 7 July 1914.

54 Wright, op. cit., p. 216.

55 See S. A. Harris, 'The Old Bluecoat Hospital, Liverpool'. Was it designed by Thomas Ripley?', *Transactions of the Historic Society of Lancashire and Cheshire,* Vol. 109, 1957.

56 Reilly, op. cit. in note 9, p. 132; *The Builder,* Vol. 85, 1903, p. 364, noted that the building 'will shortly be pulled down'.

57 Copies of the undated appeal, University of Liverpool Archives, 4A/3/4; one copy, however, is attached to a letter of explanation by Reilly dated 28th April 1908; MacCunn, op. cit., p. 3; Wright, op. cit., p. 55.

58 Reilly, op. cit. in note 9, p. 132.

59 *Viscount Leverhulme,* pp. 255–56.

60 See illustration of this in *The Builder,* Vol. 125, 1923, p. 100; *Journal of the Royal Institute of British Architects,* Vol. 17, 1910, p. 694; referred to the shock of the 'changed name [which] rather ruthlessley destroys association with the past'.

61 Reilly, op. cit. in note 9, p. 135; *Viscount Leverhulme,* p. 139; University of Liverpool Archives, various letters, D/207/2/3.

62 See plans: *The Building News,* Vol. 98, 1910, p. 509; *Journal of the Royal Institute of British Architects,* Vol. 17, 1910, p. 584; University of Liverpool Archives, 4A/3/6 plans.

63 *Journal of the Royal Institute of British Architects,* Vol. 17, 1910, p. 694; *The British Architect,* Vol. 74, 1910, pp. 2, 33.

64 University of Liverpool Archives, 4/1/23, letters from Reilly to the Vice Chancellor, 8 July 1911 and 21 January 1913.

65 University of Liverpool Archives, S3210, letter from Reilly to Lever, 24 September 1912.

66 Liverpool University Archives, 4/1/23, letter from Reilly to the Vice Chancellor, 21 January 1913.

67 *The Builder*, Vol. 108, 1915, p. 429; Royal Academy, op. cit., p. 195; L. B. Budden, op. cit., pp. 67–68. Bradshaw had been a Lever prize winner in 1913 and was to be the first Rome scholar. Later he became secretary of the Royal Fine Art Commission. See also Kelly, op. cit., pp. 227–29.

68 *Progress*, Vol. 33, 1933, pp. 74–78.

69 Unilever House Archives, letter from Lever to Professor Carey, 24 June 1914.

70 See *Journal of the History of Collections*, Vol. 4, 1992, p. 180.

71 See Wright, op. cit., p. 63; University of Liverpool Archives, 4A/3/5, letters Hugh Rathbone to Reilly, 24 January 1922; Reilly to Hugh Rathbone, 27 January 1922. I am grateful to Dr Helen Power of the School of Tropical Medicine for discussing with me the results of her researches on the dispute.

72 W. H. Lever, *The Six Hour Day*, 1918, p. 223. Reprint of an address by Lever to the Liverpool Literary and Philosophical Society in 1917.

73 A. R. Allan, *The Building of Abercromby Square*, 1986, p. 30.

74 Liverpool University Archives, S3211, letter from Reilly to Lever, 12 November 1912.

75 In fact, T. F. Shepherd and E. L. Bower, though Naseby Adams had initially been mentioned with Bower as architect for the proposals. See MacCunn, op. cit., pp. 4–5, 8–9; Liverpool University Archives, S3211, letter from Reilly to Lever, 17 September 1913.

76 Liverpool University Archives, S3212, letter from Reilly to Mrs. Calder, 6 March 1914.

77 Ibid., Reilly to Lever, 10 March 1914.

78 See MacCunn, op. cit., pp. 10–11, 76–77; letter from Clifford Muspratt to Lever early April 1914.

79 MacCunn, op. cit., pp. 78–84.

80 Edward Morris, 'Paintings and Sculpture' in Royal Academy, op. cit., pp. 26–27.

81 After Lever's death, Reilly made inquiries about whether the School could move back into the Bluecoat School. See Unilever House Archives EL/1/20 and EL/6/11.

82 See Royal Academy, op. cit., p. 156, for some of the many references to this.

83 Ernest Prestwich interview, 7 August 1974.

84 Interview with James Lomax-Simpson, 24 March 1971. Lomax-Simpson said then that he believed Lever lost interest in Liverpool after disagreeing with the University.

85 Liverpool University Archives, 4A/3/5, letter from Reilly to the Vice Chancellor, 8 January 1912.

86 *The University of Liverpool, Calendar*, 1916, pp. 502–03.

87 *Architects Journal*, Vol. 61, 1925, p. 728. See also Wright, op. cit., p. 31.

88 Simon Pepper and Mark Swenarton, 'Neo-Georgian Maison-type' in *Architectural Review*, Vol. 168, 1980, pp. 87–92. For some references to Lever's changing thoughts on industrialised building techniques, see *Journal of the History of Collections*, Vol. 4, 1992, p. 182. Lever had a long interest in cheaper cottage building techniques and had been a patron of the Cheap Cottages Exhibition held at Letchworth in 1905 and was actively involved with the Yorkshire and North Midlands Model Cottage Exhibition, held in Sheffield in 1907.

89 Lionel Budden (ed.), *The Book of the Liverpool School of Architecture*, 1932, p. 47; *The Builder*, Vol. 125, 1923, p. 63; *Progress*, Vol. 23, 1923, p. 184.

90 C. H. Reilly, *Representative British Architects of the Present Day*, 1931, p. 16. See also the appreciation of Reilly by S. C. Ramsey in *The Book of the Liverpool School of Architecture*, pp.

25–28, for an account of Reilly's changing tastes, and Lionel Budden, 'Charles Reilly, An Appreciation' in *Journal of the Royal Institute of British Architects*, Vol. 55, 1948, pp. 212–13.

91 Liverpool University Archives, 4A/3/5, letter from Reilly to Hugh Rathbone, 27 January 1922.

92 Liverpool University Archives, 4A/3/4, letter from Lever to the Vice Chancellor, 11 August 1909.

93 T. H. Mawson, *Bolton: A Study in Town Planning and Civic Art*, 1910.

94 *The British Architect*, Vol. 87, 1916, p. 17. The Department may have made a model of Port Sunlight, however, for Lever—possibly for use at the 1914 Liverpool Town Planning Conference. See Liverpool University Archives, S3212, letter from Reilly to Lever, 5 May 1914; *Journal of the Royal Institute of British Architects*, Vol. 21, 1914, pp. 378–79.

Catalogue of Exhibits

The following abbreviations are used in the catalogue entries and in the biographies which follow:

A & BJ	*Architect and Builders' Journal*
A & BN	Architect and Building News
AJ	Architects' Journal
Arch. Rev.	*Architectural Review*
Art Sheds	*The Art Sheds 1894–1905*, exhibition catalogue, Walker Art Gallery, Liverpool, 1981
BLSA	Lionel B. Budden (ed.), *The Book of the Liverpool School of Architecture*, 1932
Holford	Gordon E. Cherry and Leith Penny, *Holford—a study in architecture, planning and civic design*, 1986
JRIBA	*Journal of the Royal Institute of British Architects*
Lord Leverhulme	*Lord Leverhulme, Founder of the Lady Lever Art Gallery and Port Sunlight on Merseyside, A Great Edwardian Collector and Builder*, exhibition catalogue, Royal Academy, London, 1980
LUA	Liverpool University Archives
NMGM	National Museums and Galleries on Merseyside
RIBA	Royal Institute of British Architects
SIS	Charles Reilly, *Scaffolding in the Sky, a semi-architectural autobiography*, 1938
SLSB	Charles Reilly, *Some Liverpool Streets and Buildings in 1921*, 1921

All measurements are in centimetres, height before width. Measurements of books and reprints of photographs are not given.
The support is paper unless otherwise specified.

1.
Robert Anning BELL, 1863–1933
Poster for Liverpool School of Architecture and Applied Arts, 1894
Lithograph in three sections, 77 X 81.5, 104.5 X 81.5 and 99 X 81.5

Bell was instructor in drawing and painting at the Liverpool School of Architecture and Applied Arts (the Art Sheds) from autumn 1894 to summer 1898. The style of his poster shows the School's allegiance to the Arts and Crafts movement under its first Professor of Architecture, Frederick Moore Simpson.

Ref. *Art Sheds*, cat. 21.

The Board of Trustees of the National Museums & Galleries on Merseyside: Walker Art Gallery

2. (Fig. 25)
Frederick Moore SIMPSON, 1855–1928 (architect)
Charles John ALLEN, 1862–1936 (sculptor)
Unveiling of the Queen Victoria Monument, Derby Square, Liverpool, 27 September 1906
Photograph

The monument was designed by Reilly's predecessor as Roscoe Professor of Architecture, with sculpture by the head of Sculpture and Modelling at the School of Architecture and Applied Arts. Reilly was not impressed, describing the dome as being 'half on and half off its columns'; he thought it 'a pity that so much fine modelling has been expended on such a poorly placed and poorly conceived whole' (*SLSB*, p. 32).

Ref. *Art Sheds*, cat. 13.

The Board of Trustees of the National Museums & Galleries on Merseyside: Walker Art Gallery

3. (Fig. 26)
Stanley PEACH, 1858–1934 and
Charles Herbert REILLY 1874–1948
The Central Electric Company's Station, Grove Road, London
Photograph of a watercolour by Stanley Adshead, reproduced in *The Building News*, 21 November 1902.

Stanley Peach, a London architect specialising in the design of electricity generating stations, took Reilly on as his partner c.1900. According to Reilly,

Fig. 25 (Cat. 2)

Fig. 26 (Cat. 3)

Peach 'was a good constructor but diffident about his own powers of design. The result was that he tried far too hard to dress up his engineering buildings, with their fine roofs and great chimneys, with 'architecture' when they would have been much better left alone. I am afraid I was perfectly ready to help in this nefarious business. The great chimney overlooking Lords' cricket ground, built square instead of round and turned into a campanile, is a result. There were to be six of these in a row, the central station below them being intended to supply current in bulk to half London. If these six great towers had been put up they would have been rather fine dominating the northern entrance to the town, but finer still if they had been left plain' (*SIS* p. 56). After his successful interview for the Roscoe chair at Liverpool, Reilly heard that 'it was a drawing of the six great chimneys for the central electric station outside Lords' cricket ground which had most impressed the University committee' (*SIS* p. 65)—presumably the drawing reproduced here.

Refs. C. S. Peach, 'Notes on the Design and Construction of Buildings Connected with the Generation and Supply of Electricity, Known as Central Stations', *JRIBA*, 1904, pp. 278–318; Glynne Boyd Harte and Gavin Stamp, *Temples of Power*, 1979; A. Stuart Gray, *Edwardian Architecture: A Biographical Dictionary*, 1985.

British Architectural Library Photographs Collection, Royal Institute of British Architects

4. (Fig. 27)
Charles Herbert REILLY
Generating station, laundry, and associated buildings, Lyme Park, Cheshire, 1904–05
Photograph

This was a project which Reilly brought with him from Peach's office to Liverpool. There is extensive correspondence about it in Reilly's letter books from 20 April 1904 onwards; on 13 November 1905 he mentioned having photographs taken of the engineer's residence and workshops, which were presumably complete by then (LUA, D207/2/1). The style, materials and grouping of these buildings are entirely in the Arts and Crafts manner, but it is possible that in this Reilly was following the demands of his patron at Lyme, Lord Newton. An alternative, unexecuted scheme signed by Reilly and datable to before 20 January 1903, proposed a symmetrical arrangement around a courtyard with classical details (The National Trust, Lyme Park archives, LP 1440). On 8 November 1904 Reilly wrote to the Vice Chancellor of the University, informing him of the job he was doing at Lyme and saying that he thought it was good for his students to be able to see 'real work in the course of execution' (LUA, D207/2/1).

Fig. 27 (Cat. 4)

5. (Fig. 2)
Charles Herbert REILLY (architect)
Stanley Davenport ADSHEAD, 1868–1946 (perspectivist)
Competition design for Liverpool Cathedral: exterior, 1902
Pencil and watercolour, 105.7 X 85

Reilly entered the competition for the design of Liverpool Cathe,dral while working as a lecturer in architecture at King's College, London, and collaborating with Stanley Peach. The terms of the competition aroused controversy by specifying that entries should be in the gothic style. According to Reilly, his was 'the only classical design to be commended by the assessors, Norman Shaw and Bodley, so it may be said to have led the classical competitors who were nearly half the list' (*SIS*, p. 65). This perspective of the exterior and one of the interior (see cat. 6) were commissioned by Reilly from Stanley Adshead, whom he had met while working in the office of John Belcher. A drawing of the cathedral's main entrance by Reilly himself, now with the RIBA (Jill Lever (ed.), *Catalogue of the Drawings Collection of the Royal Institute of British Architects, O-R*, 1976, p. 114), shows his own weakness as a draughtsman which Adshead's brilliant watercolours served to offset. Reilly claimed that no plan of the cathedral site was provided to entrants, and that when he came to Liverpool to deliver his completed drawings he visited St James's Mount and realised his 'vast classical design with a dome was no good' (*SIS*, p. 65). The two perspectives were shown at the Royal Academy in 1903, and the St Louis exhibition in 1904. They subsequently hung on the walls of the Liverpool School of Architecture.

University of Liverpool Art Gallery and Collections

6.
Charles Herbert REILLY (architect)
Stanley Davenport ADSHEAD (perspectivist)
Competition design for Liverpool Cathedral: interior, 1902
Pencil and watercolour, 122.3 X 79.4

Stanley Ramsey, Adshead's partner from 1911, recalled seeing him at work on this drawing in Peach's office: 'I saw a tall, thin man in front of an enormous drawing on an easel flicking in shadows with the aid of a long straight edge, and whistling in a loud but uncertain key . . . The drawing in question was the interior of the Cathedral—one of the finest Adshead ever made' ('Our Work Together', type-script, c.1946).

University of Liverpool Art Gallery and Collections

Fig. 28 (Cat. 7)

7. (Fig. 28)

Victoria Building, Liverpool University: exterior

Photograph, from *City of Liverpool Handbook Compiled for the Congress of the Royal Institute of Public Health*, 1903

When Reilly arrived in Liverpool as the newly-appointed Roscoe Professor of Architecture his department was housed in Alfred Waterhouse's Gothic Revival Victoria Building of 1887–92. He found its combination of medieval asymmetry and harsh Victorian materials, especially glazed terracotta, repugnant. 'The . . . founders of University College', he later wrote, had chosen to go 'to the fashionable architect of the day and accept his recipe: Gothic, because it gave a scholastic air; French—though less stress was probably laid on that—because it was different from the older universities, and allowed a greater number of storeys; but, most important of all, hard and sanitary, guaranteed never to show any signs of wear' (*SLSB*, pp. 62–63).

University Archives, University of Liverpool

8. (Fig. 29)

Victoria Building, Liverpool University: interior of Department of Architecture, Modelling (Ornament) Room

Photograph, from *City of Liverpool Handbook Compiled for the Congress of the Royal Institute of Public Health*, 1903

Reilly wrote of the room where he began his teaching career at Liverpool: 'The walls of the . . . architectural studio . . . were hung with plaster casts of gothic ornament . . . These casts were very indicative of the time and were really an inheritance from Ruskin's teaching. Ornament was architecture and if one wanted to be an architect one had to know by heart the traditional ornament of the particular style then in the ascendant. As that altered and another past style was revived so were the casts in the two or three architectural schools then existing. I myself at once began putting away the gothic casts and putting the Renaissance and classical ones into positions of greater prominence, and even buying new' (*SIS*, pp. 70–1).

University Archives, University of Liverpool

9.

Charles Herbert REILLY

Scheme of New Buildings for the Faculties of Arts and Fine Arts for the University of Liverpool, 1905

Illustration in *The Builder's Journal and Architectural Record (Supplement)*, 18 October 1905

This design is connected with two ambitious schemes in which Reilly tried to interest the soap manufacturer William Hesketh Lever, with a view to securing his financial help: the removal of the University's Faculty of Arts to a new building on the Old Haymarket site (where the entrance to the first Mersey Tunnel now is), and the setting up of a new Faculty of Fine Arts with Chairs to be held by Augustus John, Epstein and Elgar among others (*SIS*, pp. 123–5). The design, like Reilly's later entry for the London County Hall competition, borrows its twin domes from the Royal Naval Hospital at Greenwich. It was exhibited at the Royal Academy in 1905; a letter from Reilly was published in *The Builder*, on 20 May, apologising for its unconscious plagiarising of a design by E. A. Rickards (1872–920), an architect he greatly admired.

City of Liverpool Libraries and Information Services: Central Library

10.

Charles Herbert REILLY

Sketch design for County Hall, London, 1907

Pen and ink and watercolour, 19.4 X 39.8

This rough sketch was worked up into an impressive perspective by Stanley Adshead (reproduced in *BLSA*, plate II), although perspectives could not be submitted under the terms of the competition for County Hall. The competition was won by Ralph Knott (1878–1929) with a design which Reilly considered 'a disaster for monumental architecture in England' (LUA, Reilly letter books, D207/2/2, 21 February 1908), and he entered into public debate on the subject. His own design was published in the *Building News,* 15 November 1907. In Knott's winning scheme, the great hemicycle which is the most memorable part of the design was placed on the land side. In execution it was moved to the river front, as Reilly had already proposed in his competition entry.

Refs.: Hermione Hobhouse (ed.), *Survey of London: Monograph 17,* County Hall, 1991; The Building News, 15 November 1907.

The Lady Reilly

11. (Fig. 30)
Ethel FRIMSTON
Statuette of Charles Herbert Reilly
Plaster, 50 X 20 X 12

Ethel Frimston (née Martin) studied at the Art Sheds and was an active member of the Sandon Studios Society, a lively Liverpool arts club that combined energetic socialising with the encouragement of progressive art. She joined in 1905, shortly before Reilly. She provided the sculptural decoration for Reilly's Students' Union building (*Building News*, 13 May 1910, p. 672; Liverpool Autumn Exhibition 1912, no. 2123) and urns for his laying out of Dove Park, Woolton (Sandon Studios Society Exhibition, Liberty Buildings, Liverpool, 4 March–1 April 1911).

Eric and Joanna Le Fevre

12. (Fig. 1.)
Mary 'Bee' PHILLIPS, 1883–1981
Staff and students of the School of Architecture and Applied Arts ('The Art Sheds'), c.1904
Photograph

A student at the Art Sheds from 1902 to 1905, Mary Phillips photographed groups of her fellow students and instructors each summer. Shown here on the back row, from left to right, are C. J. Allen, J. H. MacNair and Charles Reilly.

Ref. *Art Sheds*, cat. 196–202.

The Board of Trustees of the National Museums & Galleries on Merseyside: Walker Art Gallery

13.
Dingle Bank, Liverpool
Photograph

Reilly and his wife rented this early nineteenth-century house from the aunt of the Liverpool architect W. E. Willink (1856–1924). It exactly matched Reilly's taste for the quiet elegance of Regency domestic architecture: 'it was seventy or eighty years old, and had little touches of Strawberry Hill Gothic outside, such as drip moulds over the windows, which at first rather worried my youthful professional taste, but which really did no harm and were even a little piquant and interesting. Inside it had delightfully proportioned rooms, elegantly finished with little cornices, gently moulded but with no tiresome enrichments and no circular wreaths in the centres of the ceilings' (*SIS*, p. 98). Occupied by Reilly, it became a setting for

Fig. 29 (Cat. 8)

Fig. 30 (Cat. 11)

bohemian parties, and the interior was decorated accordingly: '. . . in those days some of the things we did, such as having to our dining room a pillar-box red ceiling with varnished black cornice and brown packing paper walls, were considered rather strange and daring' (*SIS*, pp. 102–3).

University Archives, University of Liverpool

14. (Fig. 21)
Liberty Buildings: exterior
Photograph of a drawing by Stanley Adshead and Harold Chalton Bradshaw, reproduced in the prospectus of the School of Architecture for the Session 1910–11

The former Bluecoat School of 1716–18 is the oldest surviving building in the centre of Liverpool. In 1906, following the removal of the school to new buildings at Wavertree, it was put up for sale and threatened with demolition. Reilly campaigned for its preservation and re-use, suggesting in a letter to the *Liverpool Post and Mercury* of 22 May 1906 that it could become a museum of pre-Victorian English domestic decorative arts: 'the extravagancies and absurdities of the so-called Art Nouveau, as seen in Liverpool, prove the need we have of such a thing'. In 1909, thanks to Reilly's efforts, William Hesketh Lever acquired a lease on the building and made it available to Liverpool University to house the School of Architecture and the newly-established Department of Civic Design, which he had also funded. The name Liberty Buildings was adopted at Lever's request.

Ref. For a full list of sources see *Lord Leverhulme*, cat. 469, p. 195.

University Archives, University of Liverpool

15. (Fig. 22)
Liberty Buildings: interior of studio, 1910
Photograph

The former chapel of the Bluecoat School served as the principal studio.

University Archives, University of Liverpool

16.
Norman Sykes LUNN, 1908–92
School of Architecture, Ashton Street: working drawings, 1926/27
Pen and ink on paper, 97 X 64

In 1918 Lever sold Liberty Buildings and the School moved to a former hospital building in Ashton Street. The two-storey central block was used for administra-

Fig. 31 (Cat. 17)

tion, the former wards for studios. The meanness of the architecture gave rise to the affectionate nickname 'Reilly's Cowshed', but Reilly described it more appreciatively as 'a little low Georgian building . . . very insignificant at first glance, but with a certain reticence and character . . . there is no struggle anywhere for effect; everything is of the right size and at the right level, even to the door handles' (*SLSB*, p. 67). For Gordon Stephenson, one of the virtues of the building was that the studios were interconnected, so that students in the lower years learned from the comments and criticisms of their seniors (Gordon Stephenson, *On a Human Scale: A Life in City Design*, 1992, p. 18).

By kind permission of Mrs N. S. Lunn

17. (Fig. 31)
School of Architecture, Ashton Street: interior of studio, 1930
Photograph

University Archives, University of Liverpool

18.
Edwin Maxwell FRY, 1899–1987
Autobiographical Sketches, 1975
Book

For Maxwell Fry the heart of the School was its library, with an outstanding collection of illustrated books on classical architecture, ancient and modern, by Letarouilly, Choisy, Piranesi and others (Maxwell Fry, *Autobiographical Sketches*, 1975, pp. 90–92). Reilly applied to the University Librarian for permission to establish this departmental library on 9 November 1909 (LUA, S3205). It was modelled on the libraries of the great contemporary American architectural practices (see C. H. Reilly, 'Some Thoughts on Modern American Architecture', *Builder*, 30 July 1920, pp. 116–17) and the American Schools of Architecture, of which Reilly wrote to Reginald Blomfield on 3 May 1909: 'the basis of each [American] school is really the library. 10,000 volumes, mostly folio, supplemented with 20,000 photographs. No wonder the schools are doing good work' (LUA, S3205).

Edward Morris

19.
Giovanni Battista PIRANESI, 1720–78
Diverse maniere d'adornare i camini ed ogni altra parte degli edifizj, **1769**
Book

Presented to the School library by Peter Jones, an Ellesmere Port industrialist whom Reilly met while working as a munitions inspector during the First World War (*SIS*, pp. 198–99). They became friends and Reilly designed additions to Jones's Georgian house, Greenbank, outside Chester (N. Pevsner and E. Hubbard, *The Buildings of England: Cheshire*, 1971, pp. 175–76). Piranesi's combination of archaeological classicism and theatricality was very much to Reilly's taste. He edited two volumes of reproductions of Piranesi's prints and lent Piranesi engravings from his own collection to hang on the walls of the School (LUA, S3205, 26 November 1909).

University of Liverpool, Library

20.
Croquis d'Architecture, **1877–78**
Book

Reilly ordered a run of back numbers of this annual publication for the School library on 8 December 1909 (LUA, S3205). It illustrates competitive designs produced by students of the Ecole des Beaux Arts in Paris.

University of Liverpool, Library

21.
Stephen WELSH, 1892–1976
Lecture notebook: *Theory of Architectural Design*
21 X 14

Contains notes on lectures by Lionel Budden and on theoretical writers such as Geoffrey Scott and Benedetto Croce. Welsh's notes on the classical orders mention the partly engaged square piers of St George's Hall, Liverpool, a motif imitated by Reilly and a number of his students (see cat. 71 and 86).

British Architectural Library, RIBA: manuscripts collection, Welsh papers

22.
Alwyn Edward RICE, 1909–79
Architectural History sketch sheets, c.1930
Pencil on paper, 42 X 53–53.5

According to Bruce Allsopp (interview, 15 June 1995) who attended the School from 1928 to 1933, sketch sheets such as these were the students' weekly 'homework' and were largely copied from Bannister Fletcher's textbook *A History of Architecture on the Comparative Method.*

E. N. Rice

23. (Fig. 32)
Alwyn Sheppard FIDLER, 1909–90
Study of the Parthenon, 1927/28
Watercolour and pencil, 113.5 x 80

The study of the classical orders had been fundamental to architectural training since the Renaissance. By the time this drawing was made the Doric order of the Parthenon had been hailed as an icon of the Modern Movement by Le Corbusier (*Towards a New Architecture*, English translation by Frederick Etchells, 1927, pp. 203–23)

British Architectural Library Drawings Collection / Royal Institute of British Architects

24.
Prospectus of the School of Architecture for the Session 1910–11

This lavish prospectus, an example of Reilly's belief in advertising and his skill as a publicist, was a direct outcome of his first visit to America early in 1909. On 21 May that year he wrote to the Registrar of the University: '. . . since visiting America and making a collection of the prospectuses of the American Schools of Architecture I have come to the conclusion that it would be well to somewhat alter the form of our own prospectus. The alteration I wish to make is the omission of the detailed regulations governing the various courses . . . & the inclusion in their place of illustrations of the actual work of the students in each year. These illustrations will explain at a glance the character of work done & be more convincing to architects than any number of printed pages. So strongly do the

Fig. 32 (Cat. 23)

American schools feel this that they all issue a separate pamphlet of illustrations which is a large and costly volume. This they distribute gratuitously. The head of the big school at Cornell told me that an issue of their illustrations increased the school numbers from under 50 to over 100 at one entry. I am proposing to provide, without cost to the prospectus, 10 half tone blocks of students' work which I have received from various periodicals which have illustrated it. I have an estimate . . . for printing the altered prospectus. For 1,200 copies they will charge £16.10.0 against £14.0.0 for the same number last year' (LUA, S3205). By June that year Reilly had decided to illustrate the prospectus in colour (ibid.). Once published, he maximised its effect by sending review copies to *The Building News* and other periodicals (LUA, D207/2/3, 27 September 1910).

University Archives, University of Liverpool

25, 26.
Charles Reilly (ed.)
Portfolio of Measured Drawings, 1906 and 1908

The restrained, dignified, classical architecture which came to typify Reilly's School was rooted in an appreciation of Liverpool's eighteenth- and early nineteenth-century buildings, more numerous in Reilly's day than in the 1990s. In his inaugural lecture as Roscoe Professor, 'Some Tendencies in Modern Architecture', Reilly praised Liverpool's Georgian housing and said that his students would study local examples of classical architecture and publish the resulting drawings (*Building News*, 12 May 1905, pp. 673–74). The two volumes of the *Portfolio of Measured Drawings* were the first result. Profits were to be used 'to help deserving students by scholarships or otherwise to travel' (LUA, D207/2/1, 8 May 1906). At the same time the volumes were exploited to attract publicity to the School, review copies being sent to the local and national press. The *Athenaeum*, unfortunately, criticised the poor quality of the printing and noted inaccuracies in the draughtmanship (*Athenaeum*, 8 August 1908). Looking back thirty years later, however, Reilly saw these publications as a water-shed: 'The obvious thing to do then, when the students had made from books and casts their studies of the classical orders, was to show a real belief in them by setting them to study on the spot their use in a particular building . . . I really think the measured drawings we published of St George's Hall were the beginning of the disproportionate influence of the little Liverpool School' (*SIS*, p. 119).

University of Liverpool, Library

27.
The Liverpool Architectural Sketch Book, **1911**

Following his appointment as Consulting Editor to the *Builder's Journal*, Reilly used his position 'not only to illustrate the fully developed classical architecture which I believed was the right thing . . . but also to publish the Liverpool School's studies of it and their designs in that manner. If it was the right thing for England to see designs of such architecture, and the Liverpool School was the only place providing them, so much the better for Liverpool' (*SIS*, pp. 119–20). Reilly cannily re-used printer's blocks made for the architectural press to offset the cost of producing *The Liverpool Architectural Sketch Book* (published in 1910, 1911, 1913 and—renamed *The Liverpool University Architectural Sketch Book*—1920). The Sketch Books contain reproductions of measured drawings of major classical buildings in Britain and overseas, and examples of design work by students. They provide a record of the School's stylistic convictions for much of Reilly's time in Liverpool.

Private collection

28.
The Liverpool Architectural Sketch Book, **1913**

Private collection

29.
The Liverpool University Architectural Sketch Book, **1920**

Private Collection

30. (Fig. 6)
Derek BRIDGWATER, 1899–1983
Six Hour Sketch: A Baldacchino, early 1920s
Pencil and watercolour, 76.5 X 56

An outstanding feature of teaching at the School was the six hour sketch, an idea taken from the Ecole des Beaux Arts. All years took part in the exercise, the subject was announced on Monday morning and the results were criticised in front of the whole School on Tuesday morning, usually by Reilly. The inscription 'Mention, C.H.R.' added to a drawing was a great accolade. A premium was put on imagination and the subjects, often fantastic, were chosen to encourage this. According to Reilly 'Mondays were for architecture in the clouds. I believe that is laughed at today [1938], but it produced results. Palaces for Kubla Khan are in my opinion a necessary part of architectural education . . . Looking back I notice, too, that the ones who did best at these impractical things, as they would seem to the modern student, are the ones who have since succeeded best in practical, everyday work such as Maxwell Fry, William Crabtree, Derek Bridgwater and Godfrey Thearle' (*SIS*, p. 209). As a first year student, Pearce Hubbard was astonsished to compare his workman-like six hour sketch of a toy theatre with the flights of fancy drawn by his seniors; he looked back on this experience as having opened his eyes to the creative possibilities of architecture (information from Richard Hubbard, 1995).

Eric and Joanna Le Fevre

31.
Alwyn Edward RICE
Six Hour Sketch: A Monument in the Mersey to Anglo Saxon Civilisation, 1931/32
Charcoal on paper, 69.2 X 101.5

E. N. Rice

32.
Norman Sykes LUNN
Six Hour Sketch: A Royal Reception Tent in a Square, late 1920s
Pencil and watercolour, 59 X 92

The square in question is Abercromby Square, Liverpool. St Catherine's church (demolished in the 1960s) is on the left.

By kind permission of Mrs N. S. Lunn

33.
Gordon STEPHENSON, born 1908
A Museum of Archaeology in a Mediterranean Country: *esquisse* 1930
Pencil, 95 X 68.8

Finalists in the competition for the Rome Prize were required to begin by producing a sketch plan, or *esquisse*, of their proposals. In the French jargon of the competition this was to be made *en loge*, in other words virtually in solitary confinement. Competitors went on to make highly finished drawings in which they were not allowed to depart radically from the original idea expressed in the *esquisse*.

University of Liverpool Art Gallery and Collections

34.
Gordon STEPHENSON
A Museum of Archaeology in a Mediterranean Country: elevation and section 1930
Pencil and watercolour, 82.5 X 120

Gordon Stephenson's sympathies lay with the European Modern Movement rather than the Beaux Arts classical tradition of which the Rome Prize was the culmination. This preference is reflected here in the application of classical architectural fragments (exhibits in the museum) to a severe, geometrical building with few mouldings and little decoration. According to Stephenson his design 'was not only influenced by the Modern Movement in Europe, but also by a deep concern about the background for archaeological displays. It seemed to me quite wrong to design a pseudo-classical building as a background for fragments of classical architecture and sculpture'; nevertheless, he modelled the general shape of his design on 'engravings in the school library of . . . Roman ruins, and especially the remains of the Thermae of Caracalla' (letter, 29 December 1995). The 1930 Rome Prize was won by Stephenson's close friend and Liverpool contemporary, William Holford (see *Holford*, pp. 23–26).

University of Liverpool Art Gallery and Collections

35. (Fig. 33)
Herbert THEARLE, 1903–71
Measured drawing of a chest, Palazzo Ducale, Urbino 1927
Pencil, 31 X 43

In 1926 Herbert Thearle was awarded the Henry Jarvis Studentship of the Royal Institute of British Architects, tenable for two years at the British School in Rome. In the winters of 1927 and 1928 he made visits to Urbino, Florence, Perugia, Pisa and Lucca, producing careful studies of fifteenth-century architectural decoration and furniture.

Jenny Rymer (Thearle)

36.
Herbert THEARLE
Italian sketchbook
Pencil and watercolour, 23.5 X 32

Jenny Rymer (Thearle)

37.
English-Italian Conversational Dictionary

Used by Herbert Thearle in Italy. Among the useful phrases written on the flyleaf are 'Have you any architectural books of the Italian Renaissance?' and 'Which is the road to Pompeii?'

Jenny Rymer (Thearle)

38.
Harold Chalton BRADSHAW, 1893–1943
Elevation of Temple of Fortune at Praeneste and its surroundings restored, 1919
Reproduction of a watercolour in the British Architectural Library Drawings Collection/Royal Institute of British Architects

Students at the British School in Rome were required, in imitation of French Prix de Rome holders, to produce a 'restoration' of an ancient building or site, a sequence of drawings showing the present state and possible original appearance of the subject. Bradshaw's restoration of the Temple of Fortune which dominated the ancient city of Praeneste (modern Palestrina) was exhibited at the Paris Salon in 1921.

39.
Charles Anthony MINOPRIO, 1900–88
Basilica of Constantine: cross section of actual state looking east, 1927
Pencil and watercolour, 59.5 X 107.5

On 15 November 1925 Minoprio wrote to Reilly from Rome, expressing the conflict between creativity and objective study which was a recurring problem for students at the British School: 'I should much prefer to do a design for a modern building based on a Roman one, than an actual restoration, but I gather from [Stephen] Welsh and others that the Faculty would not look with favour on the idea' (British School at Rome, Jarvis Student file). Reilly, however, was sympathetic, and on 19 November wrote to Evelyn Shaw, Secretary of the British School at Rome, suggesting that 'a design for a modern purpose in the Roman manner might be agreed to by the Faculty, for instance a great Roman railway station like the Americans themselves build, would be a good exercise' (ibid.). He wrote to Shaw again on 24 November with some remarks on restorations in general: 'The larger part of the value of these restorations for architectural students is in the exercise of the imagination which they call forth. The great thing is to find imaginative

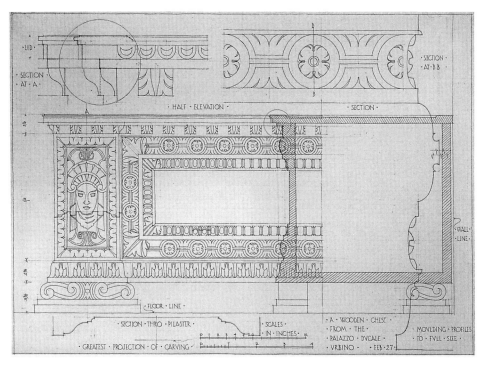

Fig. 33 (Cat. 35)

Fig. 34 (Cat. 48)

subjects such as the one Bradshaw hit upon [see cat. 38] . . . Not too much must be known of these subjects beforehand or they become archaeological exercises, and on the other hand not too little or they become flights of fancy' (ibid.). By the following March, Minoprio had decided to make the Basilica of Constantine the subject of his restoration and was helped by an archaeologist at the British School, Ian Richmond. The 1925 Rome Scholar in Sculpture, Emile Jacot, assisted with the reconstruction of the statue of Constantine (see *Papers of the British School at Rome*, vol. XII, 1932, pp. 1–25 and plates I–XIII; review by S. Rowland Pierce, *JRIBA*, 17 June 1933, pp. 635–36).

British Architectural Library Drawings Collection / Royal Institute of British Architects

40.
Charles Anthony MINOPRIO
Basilica of Constantine: restored cross-section through short axis
Pencil, 72.5 X 104.5

British Architectural Library Drawings Collection / Royal Institute of British Architects

41.
William HOLFORD, 1907–75
Piazza del Campo, Siena, 1932
Ink, pencil and watercolour, 93.5 X 115.5

From June 1932 to early 1933 Holford's work as a Rome Scholar was dominated by the study of Italian piazzas, resulting in an unpublished essay, 'The Piazza' (LUA, D147). This was both an architectural history and a statement of Holford's own views on the balancing of practical and aesthetic considerations in town planning (see *Holford*, pp. 44–46).

British Architectural Library Drawings Collection / Royal Institute of British Architects

42.
Stephen WELSH, 1893–1976
Courtyard of the Cancelleria, Rome
Pencil and watercolour, 70.5 X 58

British Architectural Library Drawings Collection / Royal Institute of British Architects

43.

Frederick Orchard LAWRENCE, 1893–1971
Temple of Jove, Ostia, c.1922
Pencil and watercolour, 90 X 105

Lawrence's work on Ostia was published in *Architettura e Arti Decorative*, September and October 1923, and *JRIBA*, 16 October 1926, pp. 597–605.

British Architectural Library Drawings Collection / Royal Institute of British Architects

44.

Alwyn Sheppard FIDLER
Church of S. Francesca Romana, Rome: elevation, 1934
Pencil, 128 X 76

John Sheppard Fidler

45.

Ecole des Beaux Arts: Concours d'Architecture de l'Année Scolaire 1920–21
Book

Bradshaw, Rowse and Harker, Architects and Development Consultants

46.

Architettura e Arti Decorative, **September 1926**
Periodical

Students at the British School were exposed to contemporary European architecture as well as the buildings of Antiquity and the Renaissance. While in Rome, Herbert Thearle obtained several copies of this periodical including one devoted to the work of its editor, the Italian neo-classicist Marcello Piacentini (1881–1961), and one to German industrial architecture. He also acquired the catalogue of the *Prima Esposizione Italiana di Architettura Razionale*, an exhibition of modern, anti-historical architecture held in Rome in 1928.

Jenny Rymer (Thearle)

47.
Lawrence WRIGHT, 1906–83
The Road to Rome or Ruin, 1926
Film

This film, made by Wright while a second year student at the School, was shown when the Liverpool MP T. P. O'Connor came to open the annual exhibition of students' work in 1926: 'T. P. O'Connor's visit was chiefly remarkable for a film of the work of the School made for the occasion by Laurence [sic] Wright. It was called "The Road to Rome or Ruin" and was a jolly skit on all we did. "T. P." had not only to see it, but to issue a certificate for it in due form as the film censor of those days' (*SIS*, pp. 290–91). The surviving print is much damaged and may be incomplete, but it includes some remarkable scenes: students are seen strike-breaking during the General Strike; clambering precariously over the steel frame of Herbert Rowse's India Buildings, with the domes of the Liver Building and Dock Board Offices in the background; and walking around the Colosseum and the Arch of Constantine. The Roman footage was probably shot by George Butling, a Liverpool student who won the Rome Prize in 1925; Wright apparently did not visit Italy until his fourth year (Lawrence Wright and His Work, *Pencil Points*, May 1931, pp. 327–42).

Piano accompaniment recorded by Robert Orledge, 21 August 1996

Video recording supplied by National Film and Television Archive of the British Film Institute; shown by permission of the Wright Family

48. (Fig. 34)
G. A. HOLMES
Design for a Monument to Admiral Dewey, 1907
Watercolour, 84.5 X 140.5

Reilly recalled how he returned from his first visit to the United States in 1909 'loaded with vast American prize drawings which I had been given or had managed to buy. One splendidly rendered set of a design for a monument to Admiral Dewey hung on the walls of the School, as a specimen of fine French architectural draughtsmanship, till I left in 1933 . . . It must be remembered that by the beginning of this century the Gothic Revival had reduced the mass of English architectural drawing to clumsy thick outline stuff which took little or no account—through the absence of cast shadows—of the most important thing in a building, its mass formation' (*SIS*, p. 123). But it was not just the style of Holmes's draughtsmanship which served as a model for Reilly's students; the type of subject was also imitated: buildings of doubtful function, dramatically sited on

Fig. 35 (Cat. 49)

rocky promontories, turn up regularly among the students' work. The taste for such exercises was later satirised by Maxwell Fry (*Autobiographical Sketches*, 1975, pp. 99–100) and Lawrence Wright (see cat. 153).

University of Liverpool Art Gallery and Collections

49. (Fig. 35)
Edward CARTER PRESTON, 1884–1965
Mind and Matter, 1920
Ink and watercolour, 59 X 47.5

A caricature contrasting the earthy, corpulent Liverpool painter Henry Carr with the cerebral Lionel Budden, Reilly's second-in-command. Budden's body is constructed out of drawing instruments and he wears an Ionic capital as a hat. On the steps of the Doric temple in the background are the names of celebrated classical architects, ascending from Ictinus and Callicrates, designers of the Parthenon, to McKim, Mead and White.

The Board of Trustees of the National Museums & Galleries on Merseyside: Walker Art Gallery

50. (Fig. 36)
Ezra Augustus WINTER, 1886–1949 and
Joseph Stanley ALLEN, b.1898
'Liverpool': mural from the New York Cotton Exchange, c. 1923
Photograph of painting on canvas, original painting approximately 630 X 300

The New York Cotton Exchange at 60 Beaver Street, in the financial district of lower Manhattan, was rebuilt as a twenty-three storey skyscraper in 1922–23 to the designs of Donn Barber. Unusually, the trading room was at the top of the building with windows on three sides giving an extensive view of New York harbour. A contemporary account describes how the room was ornamented with 'four nobly conceived mural paintings and a decorated ceiling, all the work of Ezra Winter. The paintings, typifying commerce and transportation, represent the harbors of Alexandria, Bombay, Liverpool and New Orleans, four important cotton ports. They are shown from an elevation which makes the pictures correspond to the panoramic view of New York Harbor as seen in actuality from the windows and balconies of the room. While inspiringly decorative in treatment, the paintings are the result of exhaustive studies that insure their fidelity and correctness' (*New York Cotton Exchange 1871–1923*, introduction by Edward E. Bartlett Jr, New York, 1923). J. S. Allen, recently graduated from the Liverpool School of Architecture, was working in Barber's office at this time and at his

Fig. 36 (Cat. 50) (Ezra Winter Papers, Archives of American Art, Smithsonian Institution)

request helped Winter with the murals, in particular the Liverpool one. He recalls working on the canvases in the roof space of Grand Central Station, before their installation in the Exchange (interview, 28 February 1995).

Ezra Winter Papers, The Archives of American Art, Smithsonian Institution, Washington DC

51.
Charles Reilly, 'The City of Washington and American Architecture',
***Country Life*, 18 February 1922**

City of Liverpool Libraries and Information Services: Central Library

52.
Wesley DOUGILL, 1893–1943
Scrapbook
34.5 X 24

Wesley Dougill was both a student and a teacher at the Liverpool School of Architecture. This scrapbook contains cuttings from the architectural press, mostly illustrations of American commercial and civic buildings of the type admired by Reilly.

Mrs Pat Goudie

53.
Charles Herbert REILLY
***McKim, Mead and White*, 1924**
Book

One of a series with the overall title 'Masters of Architecture', edited by Reilly's former student at King's College, London, Stanley Ramsey. This was the first monograph on the celebrated American practice to be published in Britain.

City of Liverpool Libraries and Information Services: Central Library

54. (Fig. 37)
Thomas HASTINGS, 1860–1929, with Charles Herbert REILLY
Devonshire House, Piccadilly, London, designed 1924, completed to different design 1927
Illustration in the *Year Book of the Architectural League of New York*, 1925

In his autobiography Reilly gives a colourful account of his involvement with this project (*SIS*, pp. 226–31). He was invited by J. B. Stevenson, managing director of

Fig. 37 (Cat. 54)

Fig. 38 (Cat. 57)

Holland, Hannen and Cubitts, to suggest a suitable American architect to design an apartment block to replace old Devonshire House. Reilly suggested his friend Thomas Hastings, and Stevenson appointed Hastings and Reilly as joint architects. Reilly travelled to New York to work on the scheme, taking leave from the School on the understanding that his students would be given the chance to work on the interiors of individual apartments in the completed building. But events took a different course: 'it was too big for its time. Finally two thirds of the site was sold off . . . and Stevenson went back to America to get a new scheme, which was the one actually built. That has little to do with me therefore except that by some strange luck my outline of the masses to Piccadilly survived throughout.' Along with Bush House in the Aldwych, Devonshire House is the outstanding example in London of an American classical building designed by an American architect, but this style which Reilly had promoted as modern was seen by some as out-of-date. Devonshire House was deplored by Charles Rennie Mackintosh who considered it an absurd anachronism (Glasgow University, Hunterian Museum and Art Gallery, letter from C. R. Mackintosh to his wife, 1 June 1927). Christian Barman, a former student at the Liverpool School, pointed out that it was illogical for the upper storeys to be set back in the manner of a New York building, because the American zoning regulations which determined such set backs were irrelevant to this site (Christian Barman, *Balbus, or the Future of Architecture*, c. 1926, pp. 50–51). Reilly himself had misgivings about the surface richness of the building. His nephew Sir Patrick Reilly recalls him 'complaining that [Hastings] insisted on the rather fussy decoration on the exterior of the building which Uncle Charles disliked heartily' (letter, 8 February 1996).

Private collection

55.
Charles Herbert REILLY
Letter of introduction to Paul Cret, 24 March 1931
17.8 X 11.2

The Wall Street crash of 1929 more or less ended the scheme by which Reilly sent his best students to gain experience in the offices of his American architect friends. A. G. S. Fidler, the subject of this letter, was an exception and spent the summer of 1931 working for the Philadelphia practice of Zantzinger, Borie & Medary. Paul Philippe Cret (1876–1945), a Frenchman trained at the Ecole des Beaux Arts, had been appointed professor of design at the University of Pennsylvania in 1903. He was known to Reilly through their having acted as co-assessors in the competition for the design of Canadian war memorials in France (*Times*, 23 December 1920).

John Sheppard Fidler

56.
ZANTZINGER, BORIE & MEDARY (architects)
Alwyn Sheppard FIDLER (draughtsman)
Design for a Column for the US Department of Justice building, Washington DC, 1931
Dyeline print, 100 X 61

Built between 1931 and 1934, the Department of Justice building belongs to the Washington tradition of grandiose classical government office blocks, but in its details it abandons archaeological accuracy in favour of Art Deco inventiveness, for instance in the extraordinary capitals of the giant ionic order illustrated in Fidler's drawing (see Pamela Scott and Antoinette J. Lee, *Buildings of the District of Columbia*, 1993).

John Sheppard Fidler

57. (Fig. 38)
Herbert J. ROWSE, 1887–1963 and
Arnold THORNELY, 1870–1953
India Buildings, Liverpool: elevation to Water Street, 1930
Pencil and watercolour, 73 X 92

Rowse won the competition for this great office block in 1923 while working in partnership with Arnold Thornely. The assessor was Giles Gilbert Scott. It was Rowse's first major success after his return from North America and war service and it launched his career. The debt to contemporary American commercial architecture is clear in the scale of the building—it occupies an entire city block—and in such features as the vaulted corridor containing an arcade of shops which runs through the centre of the ground floor, a later modification to the prize-winning design. The architectural treatment is American too: Italian Renaissance detail is confined to the top and bottom, with a sheer expanse of wall between. The lamps flanking the entrance are modelled on those of the Strozzi Palace in Florence. The building is of Portland stone on a steel frame and was erected in two phases. It was badly damaged in the Second World War, after which repairs were supervised by Rowse.

Refs. *AJ* 3 October 1923, pp. 491–94; 17 October 1923, pp. 562–71; 14 January 1931, pp. 44–52; *Holt's India Buildings*, volume of press cuttings in Liverpool Record Office.

Bradshaw, Rowse and Harker, Architects and Development Consultants

58.
Herbert J. ROWSE
India Buildings, Liverpool: interior of entrance hall
Photograph

The Board of Trustees of the National Museums & Galleries on Merseyside: Stewart Bale Collection

59.
Edmund C. THOMPSON 1898–1961
Maquette for sculpture of Neptune on India Buildings
Plaster, 77 X 153 X 26

The artist's daughter

60. (Fig. 39)
John Francis DOYLE, 1840/1–1913 and
Richard Norman SHAW, 1813–1912
Perspective of Royal Insurance building, Liverpool, 1897
Pencil and watercolour, 87.3 X 118.1

The Royal Insurance building was a year old when Reilly arrived in Liverpool. It was the first of a new breed of giant commercial blocks in the city which was to reach a climax in the three great buildings at the Pier Head. Though innovative in structure (it has what may be the earliest example of a steel frame in Britain) it represented for Reilly the promiscuous use of decoration and the lack of discipline in design which he saw as typical of late nineteenth-century British architecture and which he aimed to combat through his School. He thought it 'rich and impressive at first sight. Afterwards one sees that it is rather like an overgrown child. It has the details of a small building raised to a large size. The general outline of the building is that of Norman Shaw's White Star Building [in James Street], which in turn was suggested by the old German warehouses of the Hanseatic League. To this general shape has been added, on the Dale Street front, small corner turrets for defensive purposes. It is a strange conception, part of the lingering romantic sentiment of the last century' (*SLSB* pp. 43–44).

This drawing differs in some details from the building as executed. Another perspective, also different from the executed design, was shown in the 1898 Spring Exhibition at the Walker Art Gallery (cat. no. 689, plate viii).

Refs. A. Saint, *Richard Norman Shaw*, 1976, pp. 359–60; J. Newbery Hetherington, *The Royal Insurance Company's Building, Liverpool*, 1903.

The Board of Trustees of the National Museums & Galleries on Merseyside: Walker Art Gallery

Fig. 39 (Cat. 60)

Fig. 40 (Cat. 61)

61. (Fig. 40)
William Edward WILLINK, 1856–1924 and
Philip Coldwell THICKNESSE, 1860–1920, with
A. J. DAVIS, 1878–1951, as consultant (architects)
Frank RIMMINGTON (perspectivist)
Cunard Building, Liverpool, 1913–15
Watercolour, 75 X 103

The Cunard Building is the most conspicuous example of the new, refined classicism which Reilly helped to establish in Liverpool. He described it as 'probably the best commercial building in this country' (*Liverpool Daily Post and Mercury*, 24 June 1921). Its square outline and disciplined ornament make a striking contrast with the buildings on either side, the exuberant Dock Board offices and the eccentric Royal Liver Buildings. Reilly dwelt on this contrast in a lecture on 'Character in Modern Architecture' (reprinted in *SLSB*, pp. 7–18), seeing it as a glaring instance of what he considered the excessive individualism of contemporary architects, the inevitable result of there being no 'great restraining tradition' such as prevailed in the late Georgian period.

Ref. R. A. Fellows, *Edwardian Architecture: style and technology*, 1995, pp. 108–14

Gilling Dod Limited, successors to Willink and Thicknesse

62. (Fig. 19)
Charles Herbert REILLY
Cottages, 15–27 Lower Road, Port Sunlight, 1905–06
Photograph

Lever approved Reilly's plans for this block of cottages in October-November 1905 and work started at once. They were completed the following year. The crescent plan seems not to have been dictated by the site. Reilly was disatisfied with the relationship between the cottages and Lower Road, as he made clear in a letter to Lever of 27 November 1905: 'I wish my cottages could be further from the road but there is no escape from that. They look as if they ought to have a village green in front of them' (LUA, D207/2/1). The verandah of wooden trellis work, in this case taking the form of a Doric colonnade, was a favourite motif with Reilly. Adapted from early nineteenth-century examples such as decorated his own house at Dingle Bank (cat. 13), he used it in his remodelling of Belmont near Chesterfield (*Arch. Rev.*, January 1909, pp. 29–36) and in the garden he designed for Louis Cappel at 5 Ullet Road, Liverpool (*Arch. Rev.*, January 1910, pp. 26–30).

British Architectural Library Photographs Collection, Royal Institute of British Architects

Fig. 41 (Cat. 63)

Fig. 42 (Cat. 64)

63. (Fig. 41)
Charles Herbert REILLY (architect)
Stanley Davenport ADSHEAD (perspectivist)
Proposed Liverpool University Students' Union, Ashton Street, 1907
Pencil and watercolour, 58 X 54

This scheme for a Students' Union building in Ashton Street was abandoned due to objections from the nearby Royal Infirmary (see Adrian Allan and Sheila Turner, 'Si Monumentum Requiris Circumspice: A Note on the Older Plans in the Custody of the Chief Engineer', *University of Liverpool Recorder*, no. 81, October 1979, pp. 164–65). Two watercolour sketches of alternative designs, smaller and presumably earlier than cat. 63, are included in an album formerly owned by Reilly (British Architectural Library, RIBA: photographic collection). What appears to be the earliest of the three designs is in a vernacular Georgian style with Arts and Crafts touches; the later designs show Reilly adding more classical details, including the Greek masks and the pediments over the ground floor windows which can be seen in cat. 63. Ordering this watercolour from Adshead, Reilly wrote: 'I am sorry for your sake perspectives have come down in price but it suits me just now very well. Suppose you aim at a £5:5s one . . . if it serves its purpose I shall be able to afford a little more' (LUA, Reilly letter books, 7 December 1907).

Ref. *Building News*, 9 September 1907.

Eric and Joanna Le Fevre

64. (Fig. 42)
Charles Herbert REILLY (architect)
Stanley Davenport ADSHEAD (perspectivist)
Liverpool University Students' Union: Bedford Street front, 1909
Watercolour, 58.5 X 66

Following the abandonment of the Ashton Street site, Reilly redesigned his Students' Union building for a new site with entrances on Bedford Street and Mount Pleasant. The lingering vernacular Georgian details of the earlier scheme were replaced by a heavy Greek doric treatment on the Mount Pleasant facade and a more French-influenced front in Bedford Street. The change coincides with Reilly's first visit to the United States earlier in the year and his experience there of monumental American classicism. Drawings exhibited at the Royal Academy in 1909 and reproduced in *The Building News* of 29 October that year show that both facades were originally to have been doric; cat. 64, showing the Bedford Street front as built, was published in *The Building News*, 8 July 1910. The building was put up in two phases, the Bedford Street block (for men) being followed by the one in Mount Pleasant (for women), completed by 1914. A debating chamber, the Gilmour Hall, is positioned between them. The impressively austere brick side elevation originally overlooked a railway cutting (now covered), hence its relatively few windows. Inside, some rooms have classically inspired reliefs by Ethel Frimston.

Eric and Joanna Le Fevre

65. (Fig. 4)
Charles Herbert REILLY (architect)
Liverpool University Students' Union: interior of Gilmour Hall
Photograph, 62 X 51

Eric and Joanna Le Fevre

66.
***Liverpool University Students' Union*: commemorative booklet, 1914**
Inscribed 'To my friend and assistant H. A. Dod with many thanks for his help over this building. C. H. Reilly 30 March 1914'.

Harold Dod trained under Reilly and was a lecturer at the School from 1912 to 1914.

Gilling Dod Limited

67. (Fig. 3)
Charles Herbert REILLY
Church of St Barnabas, Shacklewell Lane, Dalston, London: interior
Photograph

The church was built to serve the Merchant Taylors' School Mission in the East End of London. Reilly was an old boy of the School and this is no doubt how he came to be appointed as architect. The foundation stone was laid on 3 July 1909 and the building was opened the following year. Writing in 1938, Reilly looked on St Barnabas's as the building he wished to be remembered by (*SIS*, p. 113). Its austerity would have suited the modernist taste to which he was by then committed. The style is round-arched but not explicitly classical, the materials brick and reinforced concrete, and there is virtually no ornament.

Refs. *A & BJ*, 14 September 1910, pp. 276–81; *Arch. Rev.*, September 1910, pp. 122–25

68.
Herbert Tyson SMITH, 1883–1972
Model of rood, Church of St Barnabas
Plaster, 47 X 25 X 8.5

When the church opened in 1910 the choir screen of four Roman doric columns supported a simple wooden cross. A plaque records that the screen was 'completed' in memory of Jane Denby (died 21 June 1934) and her grandchildren; this seems to refer to the setting up of the rood which now surmounts the screen. It was made by the Liverpool sculptor Herbert Tyson Smith in 1936, according to Roderick Bisson (*The Sandon Studios Society and the Arts*, 1965, p. 84). Cat. 68 appears to be a small-scale replica of the rood rather than a preparatory model for it. Tyson Smith also made two impressive nickel candlesticks which stand on the sanctuary floor (*The Studio*, Vol. 86, 1923, p. 112).
Mrs M. E. Velarde

69.
Charles Herbert REILLY
Notebook, 1909 etc.
25.5 X 20

Contains sketch plans of the site of the Students' Union and of Holy Trinity church, Wavertree, the latter dated December 1909.
University Archives, University of Liverpool

70. (Fig. 43)
Charles Herbert REILLY
Holy Trinity church, Wavertree, Liverpool: chancel interior
Photograph

Reilly was invited to make alterations to this church by the incumbent, Mr Mitchell, who was also a personal friend. A plan of Reilly's scheme dated 23 November 1910 is in the Liverpool Record Office (283 DIO 251/117). The completed work, which entailed removing the galleries on either side of the body of the church and extending the building eastward to form a new chancel, was consecrated on 1 December 1911 (Jim Schroeder, *The Life and Times of Wavertree Parish Church of the Holy Trinity 1794–1994*, 1994). The chancel is separated from its flanking vestries by square piers, engaged below but freestanding above, a motif adapted from the exterior of St George's Hall. A review of the building in the *Manchester Guardian*, 15 December 1911, describes the original decoration of the new chancel: 'the colour scheme of red and drab, with the pews and woodwork black, entirely justifies itself. The expense has been large—over £5,000.'

Fig. 43 (Cat. 70)

71. (Fig. 44)
Charles Herbert REILLY
Design for a Church of Humanity, Liverpool
Lithograph, 38 X 25.2. Extract from *The Builder*, 15 May 1911.

This design was commissioned from Reilly by Edmund Rathbone, himself an architect and a member of the Positivist Church—or Church of Humanity—a sect which followed the teachings of Auguste Comte and which enjoyed some success in Liverpool. Reilly's proposals were published in the *Architectural Review* (March 1911, pp. 148–50) with accompanying text by Rathbone. The plans reflect Positivist liturgy and beliefs, with chapels devoted to 'thirteen great exemplars of Humanity's past providence' (Homer, Dante, Descartes, etc.), and an immense cult statue of Humanity represented as a mother and child. The design is essentially an elaboration of St Barnabas's, with rich Greek Revival detailing. It was not carried out. In 1914 the Liverpool Positivists built a church in Upper Parliament Street to the designs of W. H. Ansell (Nikolaus Pevsner, *The Buildings of England: South Lancashire*, 1969, p. 482).

University Archives, University of Liverpool

72.
Stanley Davenport ADSHEAD
Liverpool Playhouse, Williamson Square: interior of auditorium
Photograph

Reilly was one of the chief movers in establishing the Liverpool Repertory Theatre as a company producing serious plays for thoughtful audiences (*SIS*, pp. 140–1; Grace Wyndham Goldie, *The Liverpool Repertory Theatre 1911–1934*, 1935). The former Star Theatre in Williamson Square was acquired as its home in 1910, Adshead was appointed architect for the necessary alterations, and the remodelled theatre opened on 11 November 1911. Reilly described the changes: 'The old auditorium was a sort of seraglio with half a dozen Moorish boxes on either side. Now it is in a large scale dignified Roman manner with two big boxes only and a ceiling with the loves of Jupiter painted in large roundels by our Sandon Studios friends at, I remember, thirty shillings a Jovian amour' (*SIS*, pp. 150–51).

Ref. *Builder*, 16 August 1912, pp. 202–03

The Board of Trustees of the National Museums & Galleries on Merseyside: Stewart Bale Collection

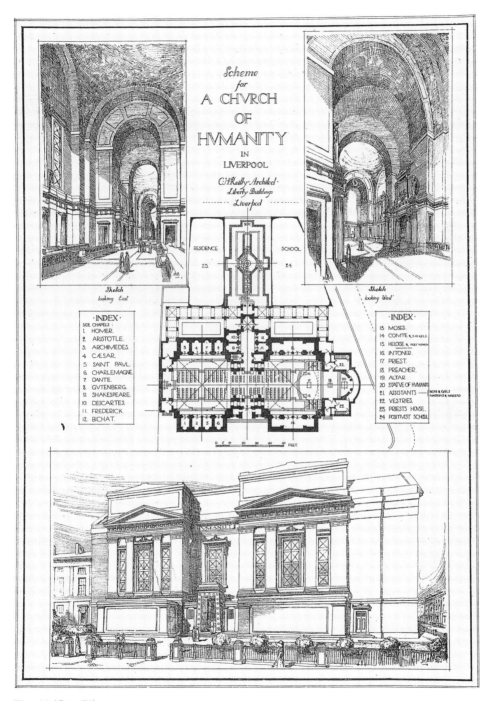

Fig. 44 (Cat. 71)

73. (Fig. 45)
Stanley Davenport ADSHEAD
Proposed building for Liverpool University, 1910
Pencil, watercolour and gouache, 28.6 X 49.3

One of a number of imaginative schemes drawn by Adshead shortly after coming to Liverpool to run the Department of Civic Design within the School of Architecture in 1909, and intended to stimulate debate about the future development of the city. This building was proposed for the site of the Liverpool Workhouse, later occupied by the Roman Catholic cathedral.

Ref. *Town Planning Review*, vol. 1, no. 2, July 1910, pp. 87–99.

The Board of Trustees of the National Museums & Galleries on Merseyside: Walker Art Gallery

74. (Fig. 23)
Charles Herbert REILLY (architect)
Harold Chalton BRADSHAW (perspectivist)
Proposed new building for Liverpool School of Architecture, 1914
Pencil and watercolour, 63.5 X 86.5

This proposal, designed for a site in Bedford Street, remained unbuilt. It is heavily influenced by the 1904 Harvard School of Architecture building by McKim, Mead and White. A reviewer in the *Building News* (30 April 1915, p. 486) noted that among the names of celebrated architects inscribed on tablets below the windows 'Elmes alone serves to represent the 19th century in England, no gothicist being so much as named or worthy. The outlook of such a school must be narrow, judged by this choice, though Le Duc is included.'

Refs. For a full list of references see *Lord Leverhulme*, cat. 474, p. 195.

University of Liverpool Art Gallery and Collections

75.
Charles Herbert REILLY
8 Buckingham Street, Westminster: interior of hall
Watercolour, 46 X 40.5

Reilly remodelled this eighteenth-century house internally and externally in 1916. 8 Buckingham Street is not in Kelly's Directory for 1916 but appears the following

A New University with a facade on public gardens and an open "Place"

Fig. 45 (Cat. 73)

Fig. 46 (Cat. 76)

year as the address of Robert Nicholas Roskell. Shortly afterwards it was occupied by the newspaper proprietor Lord Northcliffe, who described it as 'small but exquisite' (R. Pound and G. Harmsworth, *Northcliffe*, 1959, p. 535), and Reilly was proud enough of this association to mention it in a letter of December 1919 to the University Treasurer, in which he complained about not being given the chance to do more architectural work for the University (quoted in *University of Liverpool Recorder*, no. 81, October 1979, p. 164). In an article about the house (*A & BJ*, 2 August 1916, p. 50) Reilly was reported as saying he had made use of standard Georgian mouldings and enrichments manufactured by George Jackson & Sons, and he drew attention to this remark when he sent a copy of the article to his wife: 'Don't you think this was rather a brave thing to say, when everyone prides themselves on designing everything? There is much too much designing nowadays, I think, and too little acceptance of standard patterns' (RIBA Drawings Collection files). The house survives but Reilly's work has been destroyed.

British Architectural Library Drawings Collection / Royal Institute of British Architects

76. (Fig. 46)
Edgar QUIGGIN and
Ernest GEE
Housing, Muirhead Avenue, Liverpool, 1920s
Photograph

Reilly saw the influence of Stanley Adshead in this type of neo-Georgian public housing of the inter-war years: 'I trace, as is indeed obvious, a great deal of the new standard of small house design in the better post-war housing schemes to the work of Adshead and Ramsey at Kennington, Dormanstown and elsewhere . . . I think it may safely be said, for instance, that the adoption in such buildings of the Georgian sash window, and its alteration from the long mansion form to the square cottage proportion, was due to them. Indeed they may claim to have ensured for the working man some of the civilities of Georgian architecture in place of the rusticities to which romantic good-natured people would have condemned them' (C .H. Reilly, *Representative British Architects of the Present Day*, 1931, pp. 25–26).

For a discussion of the role of the Liverpool School in promoting the neo-Georgian model for social housing see: S. Pepper and M. Swenarton, 'Neo-Georgian maison type', *Arch. Rev.*, August 1980, pp. 87–92.

77.
Harold Hinchliffe DAVIES, d.1960
The Rose of Mossley public house, Rose Lane, Liverpool, 1926
Photograph album, 38 X 47

Davies specialised in the design of hotels and public houses, applying to them the refined classicism he had learned under Reilly. Reviewing an exhibition which included examples of Davies's work, Reilly wrote: 'One Liverpool brewer, who was much more than a brewer, once said to me Mr Davies's public houses were so beautiful he had hopes of the middle classes taking to drink . . . One suburban public house of his is of so balanced and chaste a design I took it for an art gallery' (*Liverpool Post and Mercury*, 12 May 1930).

Merseyside Record Office

78.
Harold Hinchliffe DAVIES
The Gardeners' Arms public house, Broad Green, Liverpool, 1924–25
Photograph album, 38 X 47

Ref. Frederic Towndrow, 'Some New Public Houses in Liverpool', *AJ*, 2 June 1926, pp. 749–58.

Merseyside Record Office

79. (Fig. 47)
Edward Chambré HARDMAN 1898–1988 (photographer)
L. G. HANNAFORD and
Herbert THEARLE (architects)
Williamson Art Gallery, Birkenhead
Photograph, 20 X 25.3

The results of the competition for the Williamson Art Gallery were announced in the local press on 27 February 1926. The assessor was Robert Lorimer. Both Hannaford and Thearle were at this time in the Liverpool office of Briggs and Thornely, Hannaford having previously been a pupil of Lutyens. The architects were said to have described their design as being in the 'modern American style' (*Birkenhead News*, 27 February 1926), and like the slightly earlier Lady Lever Art Gallery it markedly resembles some contemporary American museum buildings. Thearle was only twenty-two at the time of the competition and later in 1926 went to the British School at Rome to take up the Henry Jarvis Scholarship. The building was completed in 1928.

The E. Chambré Hardman Trust

80.
George Hastwell GRAYSON, 1871–1951 and
Leonard BARNISH, 1885–1975 (architects)
Edward Chambré HARDMAN (photographer)
Lloyds Bank, Victoria Street, Liverpool, 1928–29
Photograph, 28.4 X 22

Grayson and Barnish designed branches of Lloyds Bank in Victoria Street and Bold Street, both in a crisply detailed classical style. The Victoria Street design was shown in the Liverpool Autumn Exhibition at the Walker Art Gallery in 1928 and 1929.

The architect's daughter

81. (Fig. 11)
Edward Chambré HARDMAN (photographer)
'Water Street, Liverpool, 1929'
(Martins Bank, architect Herbert J. ROWSE, under construction)
Photograph, 36.6 X 28.4

The E. Chambré Hardman Trust

82. (Fig. 12)
Edward Chambré HARDMAN (photographer)
'Water Street and Dale Street, Liverpool'
(exterior of Martins Bank, architect Herbert J. ROWSE)
Photograph, 28.6 X 20.9

In 1927, while his India Buildings was rising on the south side of Water Street, Rowse won the competition to design a new head office for Martins Bank on a site almost directly opposite. The resulting building is the outstanding example of early twentieth-century Liverpool classicism. The assessor of the competition was Reilly who through his journalism had argued strongly in favour of the North American approach to bank design. He praised the spacious, dignified banking halls of architects such as McKim Mead and White, contrasting them unfavourably with the fussy, subdivided spaces which he saw as typical of British banks: 'By calling into being the vast banking hall in all her big city banks [America] has brought about for herself a much more definite type of bank building. By deliberately avoiding this fine feature on anything like the American scale our bank buildings as a whole do not differ materially from those for any other office purpose . . . the banks of Broadway, New York, and James Street, Montreal,

Fig. 47 (Cat. 79)

Fig. 48 (Cat. 83)

Fig. 49 Martins Bank under construction, showing the travertine columns of the banking hall threaded onto the building's steel frame (British Architectural Library, RIBA, London)

form a series of architectural monuments for a comparison to which one has to go back to Italy of the Renaissance. Indeed one passes from bank to bank in an architectural pilgrimage as one does in Italy from church to church' (from a radio broadcast on Bank Architecture, c.1927, Liverpool University Archives, D.207/27). Rowse's building perfectly matches Reilly's ideal, with its top-lit, arcaded banking hall of travertine and bronze in which every detail down to the stationery holders is designed by the architect. In a lecture about the newly completed building, given before the Liverpool Architectural Society on 18 January 1933, Rowse described some of the circumstances which shaped the design. The setting back of the upper floors, determined by the right to light of adjacent properties on the west, was exploited to help prevent the building from dominating the eighteenth-century Town Hall on the east, while Renaissance detailing was also chosen out of respect for this neo-classical neighbour. Rowse claimed that 'there was no conscious striving after any particular style, but rather the treatment was the outcome of the governing conditions which were imposed' (Barclays Record Services, Group Archives, Wythenshawe: 25/162). Apart from the banking hall, the most outstanding interior is the boardroom with its painted, beamed ceiling perhaps inspired by Spanish Renaissance examples. The sculptural decoration throughout the building, mostly illustrating the twin themes of money and maritime power, is by Herbert Tyson Smith, assisted by Edmund Thompson and George Capstick. An important aspect of the building is the complete concealment of all services by means of ducting in the floors and walls, following American practice. The use of a steel frame allowed Rowse to support the walls of the light well by cantilevers, so gaining extra space on the floors above the banking hall. This device, much commented on, had been anticipated by Richard Norman Shaw in his National Westminster Bank in nearby Castle Street.

Refs. *AJ*, 7 April 1926, pp. 525–32; 18 December 1929, p. 934; 2 November 1932, pp. 543–44, 548–53, and Supplement; *Builder*, 28 October 1932, pp. 718 and 721–28; *A & BN*, 28 October 1932, pp. 102–07.

The E. Chambré Hardman Trust

83. (Fig. 48)
Herbert J. ROWSE
Martins Bank, Liverpool: interior
Photograph

The Board of Trustees of the National Museums & Galleries on Merseyside: Stewart Bale Collection

84.
Trenwith WILLS, 1891–1972 (architect)
Herbert Tyson SMITH (sculptor)
Hightown War Memorial, 1919
Photograph, 29 X 23.3

Trenwith Wills went to school at Freshfield near Hightown and lived there while studying at the Liverpool School of Architecture. He wrote to Tyson Smith on 5 August 1919, acknowledging his help in securing this commission: 'I have no doubts whatever that it is due to your efforts that my drawing has been accepted in preference to some evil gothic horror' (Tyson Smith Papers, Box 63).

City of Liverpool Libraries and Information Services: Liverpool Record Office, Tyson Smith Papers

85. (Fig. 50)
Charles Herbert REILLY (architect)
Herbert Tyson SMITH (sculptor)
Accrington War Memorial, 1922
Photograph, 28.5 X 24

Having failed to find a satisfactory design by means of a competition the Accrington War Memorial Committee sought Reilly's advice. He was asked to submit two alternative schemes, one with space for recording the names of the fallen and one without (Accrington District Central Library, War Memorial Committee minutes, 30 April and 15 June 1920). The latter was accepted by the Committee on 12 July 1920, work on site was intended to start in October, and the memorial was unveiled on 1 July 1922 (*Accrington Observer* and *Times*, 1 and 4 July 1922).

Ref. *Builder*, 22 October 1920.

City of Liverpool Libraries and Information Services: Liverpool Record Office, Tyson Smith Papers

86. (Fig. 51)
William Naseby ADAMS, c.1887–1952 and
Eric Ross ARTHUR, 1898–1981 (architects)
Herbert Tyson SMITH (sculptor)
Dewsbury War Memorial, 1923–24
Photograph, 21.5 X 29.8

Reilly acted as assessor in the competition for this memorial, the result of which was announced in the *Dewsbury District News* on 9 June 1923. The completed memorial was unveiled in September 1924 (*Dewsbury Reporter*, 6 and 13 September 1924). The square piers, embedded in the wall for half their height then silhouetted against the sky, are a striking quotation from St George's Hall, Liverpool.

City of Liverpool Libraries and Information Services: Liverpool Record Office, Tyson Smith Papers

87.
Lionel Bailey BUDDEN, 1887–1956 (architect)
Herbert Tyson SMITH (sculptor)
Birkenhead War Memorial, 1925
Photograph, 30 X 22.6

Students at the School prepared alternative designs for this memorial in 1919 (see *The Liverpool University Architectural Sketch Book*, 1920, p. 61).

City of Liverpool Libraries and Information Services: Liverpool Record Office, Tyson Smith Papers

88. (Cf. Fig. 52)
Herbert Tyson SMITH
Models for Liverpool Cenotaph relief: And the Victory that day was turned into Mourning unto all the people
Plaster, three sections 55.9 X 83.5, 55.9 X 92.7 and 55.9 X 77.1

Reilly was consulted about the site of the proposed cenotaph and responded on 22 February 1926 with the view that it should stand on the Plateau in front of St George's Hall, on the transverse axis of the Hall. To make room for it Reilly proposed that the statue of Lord Beaconsfield should be moved from this site to a position on the steps of the Hall, a suggestion which was adopted. The conditions for a competition for the design of the cenotaph were published on 3 June 1926, with Reilly named as the assessor. According to Roderick Bisson (*The Sandon Studios Society and the Arts,* 1965, p. 168) the competition attracted many entrants from the University, and on 15 October 1926 Reilly announced that the winner was Lionel Budden, his Associate Professor in the School of Architecture. The third prize went to Frederick Hamer Crossley, a former student of the School, and Herbert Thearle and John Henry Forshaw were among the others who prepared schemes. Budden's winning design (illustrated with those of other prize-winners in *The Builder,* 22 October 1926) was simplified slightly and reduced in size following the erection of a full size wood and plaster model on the site (11 May 1927), a requirement that Reilly had written into the rules of the competition (*SIS*, p. 253). However, the two long relief panels, one showing mourning civilians, the other marching soldiers, which

Fig. 50 (Cat. 85)

Fig. 51 (Cat. 86)

dominated Budden's original design were little changed. It is not clear if these were conceived independently by Budden or if the sculptor Herbert Tyson Smith collaborated in the preparation of Budden's competition entry. The two had already worked together on the Birkenhead War Memorial.

Refs. *Walker Art Gallery Annual Report and Bulletin*, Vol. V, 1974–75, pp. 30–31, with a full list of sources; Liverpool Record Office, volume of photographs, plans, press cuttings, etc., relating to the cenotaph.

The Board of Trustees of the National Museums & Galleries on Merseyside: Walker Art Gallery

89. (Fig. 53)
Charles Herbert REILLY (architect)
Herbert Tyson SMITH (sculptor)
County War Memorial, Durham, 1928
Photograph

The War Memorial stands outside the east end of the Cathedral, a site approved by the Chapter on 17 January 1925 (Dean and Chapter Minutes, Durham Cathedral). Reilly's designs were accepted by the Chapter on 3 March 1928 (ibid.) and the finished memorial was unveiled on 24 November 1928 (*Durham County Advertiser*, 29 November 1928, p. 9). It is not clear how Reilly received the commission. The Resident Architect at Durham Cathedral from 1926 to 1940 was Reginald Cordingly (1896–1962), who had been both a Jarvis Student and a Rome Scholar and would therefore have known Reilly through the British School at Rome. Reilly's design is modelled on the round Romanesque piers of the Cathedral with their incised geometrical decoration. The carving shows soldiers' kit and weaponry—helmets, shells, hand grenades, bullets, water bottles—simplified and arranged in formal patterns in a manner akin to heraldry.

The Dean and Chapter of Durham

90. (Fig. 20)
Stanley Davenport ADSHEAD
Replanning scheme for Liverpool, 1910
Pencil and watercolour, 36 X 52

One of a series of drawings made by Adshead to illustrate how Liverpool might be systematically replanned, both to enhance its appearance and improve its communications. These proposals were published in the *Town Planning Review* (vol. 1, no. 2, July 1910, pp. 87–99) and were the subject of a lecture by Adshead, organised by

Fig. 52 Liverpool Cenotaph, designed by Lionel Budden, 1926, with sculpture by Herbert Tyson Smith. Cf Cat. 88. (City of Liverpool Libraries and Information Services: Liverpool Record Office, Tyson Smith papers)

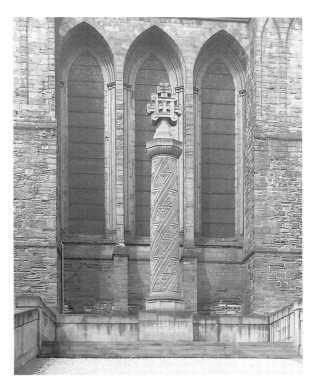

Fig. 53 (Cat. 89)

119

the Liverpool City Guild and extensively reported in the *Liverpool Courier* on 31 March 1910. Adshead's ideas were based on contemporary city planning in Germany and the United States, and involved superimposing a formal road plan on the existing haphazard layout of the city centre. At their heart was the creation of an extended river front lined with impressive new buildings, and the extension of Princes Avenue northwards as far as Lime Street to form a grand entry to the city centre from the south. In another drawing, now in the collection of the Walker Art Gallery, Adshead proposed sinking the railway tracks leading into Exchange Station under the roadway, thus improving access to the waterfront. The Old Haymarket opposite St George's Hall was identified as the site of a new Municipal Building, axially placed in relation to the Hall and the new road system.

The Board of Trustees of the National Museums & Galleries on Merseyside: Walker Art Gallery

91. (Fig. 54)
Harold Chalton BRADSHAW
Design for Liverpool waterfront, 1913
Watercolour, 68 X 116

The foreground shipping and the campanile-like skyscrapers suggest that Liverpool is here being compared with Venice, one of its great predecessors as a maritime power.

University of Liverpool Art Gallery and Collections

92.
Ernest PRESTWICH, 1889–1977 (planner)
Robert ATKINSON, 1883–1952 (draughtsman)
Scheme for completion of Port Sunlight, 1910
Illustration in T. H. Mawson, *Civic Art, Studies in Town Planning, Parks, Boulevards and Open Spaces*, 1911

In 1910 Lever held a competition among the students of the Liverpool School of Architecture and the Department of Civic Design for a revised plan for the completion of Port Sunlight Village. It was won by Ernest Prestwich, a third year student. In contrast with the informal layout of the earlier part of the Village which followed the natural lie of the land, Prestwich's scheme is a classically-conceived Beaux Arts plan. It consists of two broad vistas, The Diamond and The Causeway, intersecting at right angles, the former ending at the church from which further straight roads fan out. The formality of the plan was increased in execution, by

Fig. 54 (Cat. 91)

Fig. 55 (Cat. 99)

T. H. Mawson and J. Lomax Simpson in particular, when it was decided to position the Lady Lever Art Gallery at the end of The Diamond, further emphasising the longer of the two axes. Prestwich's scheme was shown in the exhibition held at the Royal Academy in 1910 in connection with the RIBA Town Planning Conference of that year.

Refs. *Lord Leverhulme*, pp. 155–56, with further references.

The Board of Trustees of the National Museums & Galleries on Merseyside: Lady Lever Art Gallery

93.
Stanley Davenport ADSHEAD
Replanning scheme for St Michael's Hamlet and Aigburth riverfront, Liverpool, 1909
Watercolour, 61.3 X 90.5

The area shown here includes some of the most attractive early nineteenth-century suburban villas in Liverpool: Fulwood Park, St Michael's Hamlet and Dingle Bank, where Reilly lived. Adshead's replanning scheme envisages a formal square in front of St Michael's railway station leading to a broadly symmetrical arrangement of detached houses with views of the river. The new buildings are in a quiet, elegant Regency style which takes its cue from the existing architecture of the area. In Adshead's drawing this is contrasted with the tightly packed terraces of late Victorian housing in the background. The scheme, which was illustrated in the 1909–10 prospectus of the Department of Civic Design, was not carried out. Two years later, in his work on the Duke of Cornwall's estate at Kennington, London, Adshead applied Regency elegance to the problem of working-class housing with outstanding success.

University of Liverpool Art Gallery and Collections

94.
Arthur Cecil TOWNSEND, 1896–1993
Replanning scheme for Soho, London, 1923
Pen and ink and watercolour, 46.2 X 47.4

This scheme won one of the Lever Prizes for 1923. Funded by the first Lord Leverhulme, the prizes were awarded from 1910 to 1924 'for the lay-out and architectural development of a prescribed area. The competition for the prizes open annually to Diploma and Certificate students in the Department of Civic Design and to Senior Degree and Diploma students in the School of Architecture'

(*BLSA*, p. 51). A. C. Townsend's scheme shows the intricate street pattern of Soho bisected by a curving boulevard which links Piccadilly Circus and Soho Square, while in the region of Berwick Street a semicircular *place* is made the focus of newly opened vistas and radiating streets.

By kind permission of Mr Charles Townsend

95. (Fig. 24)
John Henry FORSHAW 1895–1973
An Ornamental Park, Heswall, Cheshire, 1924
Pencil and watercolour, 94.6 X 144

Awarded the first Lever prize in the 1924 competition.

Daniel Forshaw RIBA

96.
Stephen WELSH
Civic Design lecture notebook, 1920s
22.5 X 14

British Architectural Library, RIBA: Manuscripts Collection, Welsh Papers

97 and 98.
The *Town Planning Review*, volumes 1 and 3, 1910 and 1912

City of Liverpool Libraries and Information Services: Central Library

99. (Fig. 55)
E. W. FRITCHLEY with
Srinivasarao Harti LAKSMINARASAPPA, born c1885
Blueprints for Lalit Mahal Palace, Mysore, 1918
Bound volume, 50.5 X 68.7

S. H. Laksminarasappa was Chief Architect and Engineer to the Maharaja of Mysore. The exact nature of his involvement in the construction of the Lalit Mahal Palace is unclear but is attested by his descendants. The Palace was used for accommodating the Maharaja's European guests.

The Board of Trustees of the National Museums & Galleries on Merseyside: Walker Art Gallery

100. (Fig. 56)
Frank EMLEY and
Frederick WILLIAMSON
University of the Witwatersrand, Johannesburg, 1922 onwards
Photograph

Having won the competition to design the central block of the new University of
the Witwatersrand, Emley brought in Williamson, apparently still a student at the
Liverpool School, to assist him. The symmetrical Beaux Arts plan of the campus
(dating from 1919) was matched by the monumental classicism of the architecture,
and Williamson found himself working on a project such as Liverpool students
were used to designing on paper but which few could have expected to build.
Precast concrete rather than stone was used for the facades. Work on the portico of
this building provided William Holford with his first practical experience of
architecture in 1925 (*Holford*, pp. 7–8).

Ref. Clive M. Chipkin, *Johannesburg Style—Architecture and Society 1880s–1960s*,
Cape Town, 1993, pp. 77 ff.

University Archives, University of Liverpool

101.
Albert Clifford HOLLIDAY 1897–1960
St Andrew's Church (The Scottish Memorial Church), Jerusalem, 1925–26
Photograph, 54.5 X 66

Holliday was Civic Adviser to the City of Jerusalem from 1922 and Town
Planning Adviser to the Palestine Government from 1926. He also worked in
private practice in Jerusalem. The design of St Andrew's draws on his knowledge
of the city's historic architecture and uses traditional materials, but combines these
elements in a way which is recognisably modern. On a site just below the church,
and in a similar style, Holliday built the simple, cloistered Kahn of the Order of St
John, 1926–27.

Ref. Michael Levin, 'Jerusalem Architecture During the British Mandate' in
Modern Architecture in Jerusalem, published by the Institute of Jerusalem Studies,
Jerusalem, 1980.

Paul Holliday

Fig. 56 (Cat. 100)

Fig. 57 (Cat. 104)

102. (Fig. 16)
Maurice LYON, b.1887
Headquarters of Egyptian State Telegraphs and Telephones, Cairo
Photographs

Lyon's design for this building was exhibited at the Royal Academy in 1927 (no. 1400). He was at this time Government Architect in the Ministry of Public Works in Cairo.

University Archives, University of Liverpool

103. (Fig. 17)
Philip C. HARRIS, b.1891
Sultan's Palace and Baraza (Durbar Hall), Zanzibar
Photograph

Harris was Government Architect in Zanzibar from 1922 until the early 1930s. He made various additions and alterations to the Sultan's Palace between 1926 and 1932, in a style sympathetic to the original building.

University Archives, University of Liverpool

104. (Fig. 57)
Edward William MARTIN, 1891–1977
Raskob House, Wilmington, Delaware, 1930
Photograph

Trained partly at the University of Pennsylvania and partly at the Liverpool School of Architecture, E. W. Martin returned to the United States after graduating from Liverpool in 1922. His practice was based in Wilmington, Delaware. He designed houses in the Colonial Revival style, of which the Raskob House is one of the grandest.

University Archives, University of Liverpool

105. (Fig. 58)
Herbert J. ROWSE
Proposed headquarters for Societa de Applicaciones Electricas, Plaza de Catalunya and Puerta del Angel, Barcelona, 1930
Photograph, 27.9 X 24.2

When Rowse was interviewed by a Liverpool newspaper on 30 May 1930 'he was just about to snatch a hasty dinner before catching an eight o'clock boat for

Fig. 58 (Cat. 105)

Fig. 59 (Cat. 106)

Barcelona, where he is about to put up a new building' (*Liverpool Post and Mercury*, 31 May 1930). This major commission presumably resulted from Rowse's success in the competitions for India Buildings and Martins Bank. The general form of the Barcelona design is similar to India Buildings: grand circulation spaces, public offices and shops on the ground floor with private offices and some lettable space on the eleven floors above, arranged around two light wells. The exterior combines American Beaux Arts detailing with decorative elements derived from medieval Spanish architecture. The project was abandoned, perhaps because of the deteriorating political situation in Spain. The site was acquired by the Bank of Spain, which erected a building by its own architect between 1948 and 1955 (information from Peter Holden and Bonifacio Gento Mier).

Bradshaw, Rowse and Harker, Architects and Development Consultants

106. (Fig. 59)
Harold Clayforth MASON, 1892–1960 (architect)
Cyril A. FAREY, 1888–1954 (perspectivist)
Basrah Airport, 1937
Watercolour, 53.4 X 127.2

H. C. Mason brought this commission with him when he left the post of Government Architect in Iraq and entered into partnership with J. M. Wilson in London in 1935. The airport was built alongside the Shatt al Arab to cater for the flying boats which landed there as well as conventional aircraft on the landward side of the building. Besides the normal terminal facilities it incorporated a hotel and restaurants and was among the first fully air conditioned buildings in Iraq.

Refs: C.H. Lindsey Smith, *JM, The Story of an Architect*, no date; Khalid Sultani, 'Architecture in Iraq between the two World Wars, 1920–1940', *The International Magazine of Arab Culture*, 2/3, 1982, pp. 92–105.

Wilson Mason and Partners, Chartered Architects, London

107. (Cf. Figs. 60 and 61)
Mary ADSHEAD, 1904–95
Mural from Charles Reilly's dining room, 1925, retouched 1981
Oil on canvas, laid on board; arranged as two panels, 262 X 410 and 262 X 448

This mural was commissioned by Reilly for his flat at 71 Bedford Street South, Liverpool, an early Victorian house where he lived from the mid 1920s until his retirement: 'To celebrate my wife's return I had got Mary Adshead, the daughter of my old friend Stanley Adshead, and now a distinguished artist herself, to paint a complete decoration round the walls of the little back bedroom of the original

Figs. 60 and 61 Charles Reilly's dining room at 71 Bedford Street South,
Liverpool, showing mural paintings by Mary Adshead in their original setting.
Cf. Cat. 107 (The Board of Trustees of the National Museums & Galleries on
Merseyside: Walker Art Gallery)

house, which we used as a dining room. It was a great success, the finest thing of the kind that cleverest of all our decorative painters has yet done . . . It consists of a tropical scene with a tiger jumping over the mantlepiece, a background of elephants and banana trees, a lovely negress and piccaninny, and a sort of Slade School picnic going on in the foreground. The figures, in a room about fourteen feet by twelve feet only, are nearly life-size and yet in no sense overpowering' (*SIS*, pp. 317–18). Mary Adshead considered it 'one of the best murals I ever painted, and an example of how the late 20's, early 30's did produce other things than the now popular "art deco" in interior decoration' (letter, February or March 1976, Walker Art Gallery files). The commission demonstrates both Reilly's commitment to contemporary art and his flamboyant domestic style (cf. cat. 13). When he left Liverpool in 1933 the mural went to his daughter's London house. Somewhat altered, it was bought by the University of Liverpool in 1976 and installed in the Department of Civic Design. A scale model of Reilly's dining room incorporating watercolour studies of the mural is in the University Art Collection.

Refs. *A & BN*, 8 October 1926, pp. 402–04; illustrated in colour in *The Studio Yearbook*, 1927, p. 53; Andrew W. Moore, 'University Art Collections: A Recent Acquisition', *University of Liverpool Recorder*, no. 74, April 1977.

University of Liverpool Art Gallery and Collections

108. (Fig. 62)
Alwyn Sheppard FIDLER
A Skyscraper Tower, 1929/30
Chalk on black paper, 94 X 74

Reilly was thrilled by the sight of New York skyscrapers lit up at night: 'To see brilliant windows and towers of light floating in the sky, where ordinarily one expects to see stars, means that one treads the pavement in no solemn, downcast manner. One walks on air, not knowing what to expect'(C. H. Reilly, *Some Architectural Problems of Today*, 1924, pp. 175–76). He particularly admired classically-dressed skyscrapers like the Metropolitan Life Tower of 1909 in Madison Square, and this enthusiasm is reflected in Liverpool students' designs such as those for Municipal Buildings, dated 1913, which are reproduced in the 1920 *Liverpool University Architectural Sketch Book*. Cat. 108, a six hour sketch design by an outstanding student of the late 1920s, is indebted to the next generation of New York skyscrapers, shorn of classical detail and shaped by the city's zoning laws which from 1916 required the upper storeys of tall buildings to be set back, to maintain acceptable levels of daylight.

British Architectural Library Drawings Collection / Royal Institute of British Architects

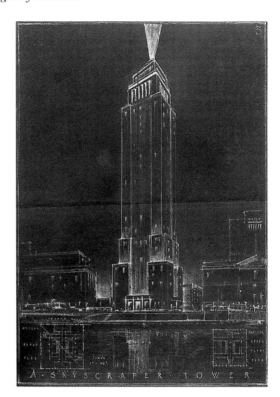

Fig. 62 (Cat. 108)

Fig. 63 (Cat. 109)

109. (Fig. 63)
Charles Anthony MINOPRIO and
Hugh Greville SPENCELY, 1900–83 (architects)
Edward Chambré HARDMAN (photographer)
Extension to the School for the Blind, Hardman Street, Liverpool, 1931
Photographs, 21.6 X 24.6, 14.5 X 28 and 24.5 X 21.5

According to H. G. Spencely's autobiographical notes (Walker Art Gallery) the architects were recommended for this commission by the Honorary Treasurer of the School for the Blind who was Spencely's bank manager. The site was previously occupied by the Church of the School for the Blind, a severe Greek Doric temple of 1818–19 designed by John Foster Jr for a site in London Road, from where it was moved here, stone by stone, in 1851. These facts are recorded in an inscription on the new building, which closely echoes the form of Foster's vanished church but with fluted pilasters instead of columns. The temple-like exterior hides an irregular plan, providing work rooms, a lounge, and a shop selling products made by the students. The style of the exterior follows the example of many contemporary buildings in North America, not abandoning classicism altogether but stripping away decorative mouldings and other projections to emphasise the underlying cubic shape. It resembles a simplified, miniature version of, for instance, Jones and Haugaard's 1928 New York State Office building in New York City. Despite the emphasis on smooth surfaces and simple masses, sculptural decoration plays an important part. The stone reliefs by John Skeaping (b.1901) illustrate crafts and other activities practised by blind people, such as piano playing, brush making, and reading braille. For the bronze doors see cat. 110 below. Reilly wrote enthusiastically to Minoprio about the building on 10 December 1931, describing it as 'strong and good and fresh and modern with interesting details—indeed with all the things one wants and so rarely finds' (family papers).

Ref. *A & BN*, 7 October 1932, pp. 8–10.

The E. Chambré Hardman Trust

110. (Cf. Fig. 64)
James WOODFORD, 1893–1976
Model of Hardman Street doors to School for the Blind, 1931
Plaster, painted to imitate patinated bronze, each leaf 305 X 77 X 14

Both Woodford and John Skeaping had been contemporaries of Minoprio at the British School in Rome, and it was while there that he formed the idea of inviting

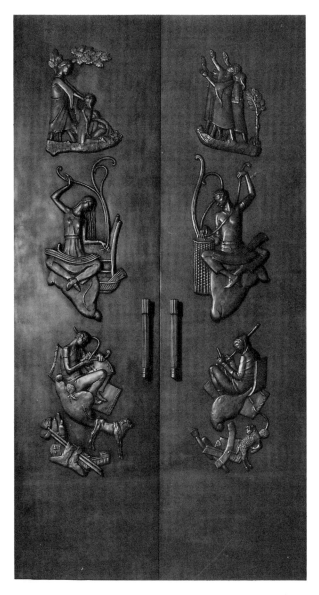

Fig. 64 James Woodford, bronze doors for the Hardman
Street entrance to the School for the Blind. Cf. Cat. 110
(Courtesy of Hugh Spencely)

them to collaborate with him on an architectural project if the opportunity arose. His stay in Italy had given him the chance to see the bronze doors of S. Zeno in Verona and of the cathedral in Ravello, about which he wrote enthusiastically (see *The Classical Tradition in British Archi,tecture*, exhibition catalogue, Building Centre, London, 1982). Woodford modelled a single leaf door for the Hope Street entrance to the School for the Blind as well as the double doors for the main Hardman Street entrance which led into the school shop. All the doors have since been moved to the School's building at Wavertree, Liverpool. The plaster models were exhibited at the Royal Academy in 1932 (no. 1483) and 1933 (no. 1605). The double doors illustrate crafts such as basket making and leather work, with New Testament scenes of Christ healing the blind. Woodford subsequently made bronze doors for two of the key British buildings of the 1930s, Norwich City Hall and the RIBA Building in Portland Place, London.

The Board of Trustees of the National Museums & Galleries on Merseyside: Walker Art Gallery

111 and 112.
Norman Sykes LUNN
Proposed Municipal Buildings and entrance to Mersey Tunnel: plan and elevation, 1931
Pencil, watercolour and metallic paint, each 94 X 61

In his final year a student at the School was required to produce a thesis, a fully worked out design solution to a complex architectural problem, presented in a series of highly finished drawings. These two sheets were part of N. S. Lunn's thesis; further drawings for the project are illustrated in *BLSA*, plates LI–LVII. As far back as 1910 Adshead had suggested that the Old Haymarket would be a fitting site for a new Municipal Building, facing St George's Hall across St John's Gardens (see cat. 90). When the Old Haymarket was proposed as the site for the entrance to the new Mersey tunnel, c.1926–27, the possibility arose of combining the tunnel entrance with a great civic building. N. S. Lunn's proposal for how this might be done—two towers and a lower linking building spanning the tunnel entrance—is one which Reilly later said he suggested to the Tunnel Committee (*Liverpool Review*, August 1934, pp. 273–75). Lunn spent his fourth year vacation in the New York office of Corbett, Harrison and MacMurray, and the detailing of his thesis design is clearly derived from the Art Deco skyscrapers he saw there. The elaborate representation of patterned floors on the plan is in line with Beaux Arts methods of draughtsmanship.

By kind permission of Mrs N. S. Lunn

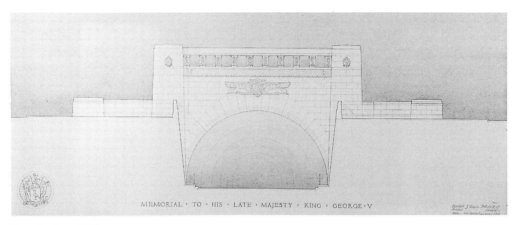

MEMORIAL · TO · HIS · LATE · MAJESTY · KING · GEORGE · V

Fig. 65 (Cat. 113)

THE · MERSEY · TUNNEL
GEORGES · DOCK · VENTILATION · & · CONTROL · STATION
LIVERPOOL

Fig. 66 (Cat. 114)

113. (Fig. 65)
Herbert J. ROWSE
Mersey Tunnel (Queensway): east elevation of Haymarket entrance
Pen and ink, pencil and watercolour, 52.5 X 100

Rowse was appointed architect to the Mersey Tunnel Joint Committee in 1931 (*The Story of the Mersey Tunnel, officially named Queensway, Liverpool*, 1934, p. 27). Reilly complained that an architect had not been involved in the project from the outset, and that Rowse's work had been compromised by decisions taken before his appointment. He particularly regretted the siting of the Haymarket entrance slightly to one side of the axis of St George's Hall, and the fact that Rowse had 'been set the impossible task of decorating what is really but a hole in the ground. The engineer too often feels he can cover up his mistakes by calling in an architect to add pretty things to hide them' (*Liverpool Review*, August 1934, pp. 273–74). In his designs for the various tunnel structures Rowse rejected the American classicism of his earlier commercial buildings in favour of a smooth, streamlined style with Art Deco ornament, also American in inspiration. The sweeping walls of the Haymarket entrance, suggesting speed and mechanical efficiency, show the appropriateness of the choice. When the former Bauhaus director Walter Gropius, newly arrived from Germany, visited Liverpool on 17–18 May 1934 he was taken through the tunnel by Rowse. His comments on the entrances and ventilating towers are not recorded, but he praised the interior with its functional dado of black glass framed in stainless steel which Rowse had also designed (*Liverpool Daily Post*, 19 May 1934, p. 6; *The Story of the Mersey Tunnel . . .*, pp. 63–65).

Bradshaw, Rowse and Harker, Architects and Development Consultants

114. (Fig. 66)
Herbert J. ROWSE (architect)
Donald BRADSHAW, 1900–71 and
George KENYON, 1908–76 (draughtsmen)
The Mersey Tunnel: George's Dock Ventilation and Control Station, Liverpool
Watercolour, 115 X 79

Rowse designed six towers to house the machinery for ventilating the tunnel, the one at George's Dock also containing administrative offices. 'All the machinery was to be in duplicate—to guard against any possibility of a failure in ventilation—and that led the way to symmetrical buildings with nicely balanced elevations' (*The Story of the Mersey Tunnel . . .*, p. 77). This tower and the one in North John Street were faced in Portland stone, in consideration of their setting in the heart of

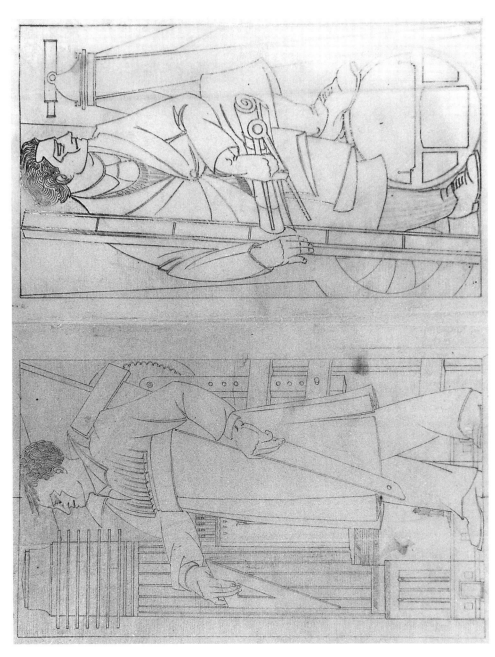

Fig. 67 (Cat. 116)

the city's business district, while brick was used for the others. Rowse's office at this date was a major employer of Reilly's graduates, and the two men responsible for this drawing, Donald Bradshaw and George Kenyon, had both trained at the Liverpool School of Architecture.

Refs. *Builder*, 18 May 1934, p. 836; *Building*, May 1934, p. 172–83; *AJ*, 3 May 1934, p. 634; *Arch. Rev.*, June 1934, pp. 202ff.

Bradshaw, Rowse and Harker, Architects and Development Consultants

115.
Jack Coburn WITHEROP, 1906–84
The Construction of Queensway
Drypoint, plate size 32.1 X 25.8

Shown in the Liverpool Autumn Exhibition, Walker Art Gallery, 1934, no 874.

The Board of Trustees of the National Museums & Galleries on Merseyside: Walker Art Gallery

116. (Fig. 67)
Edmund C. THOMPSON
Designs for relief sculptures: The Architect and The Engineer
Pencil, 40.5 X 50.5

Helped by his associate George T. Capstick, Edmund C. Thompson was responsible, under Rowse's direction, for all the carved decoration of the tunnel structures (*The Story of the Mersey Tunnel . . .*, p. 79). The greatest concentration of sculpture is on the George's Dock Ventilation and Control Station. Here, statues representing Night and Day stand sentinel over the ever-open tunnel, flanking a symbolic figure of Speed, wearing helmet and goggles. Four relief panels representing Civil Engineering, Construction, Architecture and Decoration are positioned on the north and south elevations. Cat. 116 may show alternative designs for two such panels. The Engineer rests his foot on a cross section of the tunnel and stands in front of one of its ventilating fans. Behind the Achitect are representations of the George's Dock building and the fluted column which originally stood outside the Haymarket entrance to the tunnel.

The artist's daughter

Fig. 68 (Cat. 117)

Fig. 69 (Cat. 118)

117. (Fig. 68)
Francis Xavier VELARDE, 1897–1960 (architect)
Edward Chambré HARDMAN (photographer)
Church of St Gabriel, Blackburn, 1932–3
Photographs, 11.2 X 15.5, 21.3 X 16, 24.1 X 19.2 and 24.3 X 19.2

The building committee for St Gabriel's invited Reilly to suggest a suitable architect and he recommended his former students, Velarde and B. A. Miller. Pevsner described the resulting building as 'One of the milestones in the (late) development of English church architecture towards a twentieth-century style' (*The Buildings of England: North Lancashire*, 1969, p. 65)

The E. Chambré Hardman Trust

118. (Fig. 69)
Francis Xavier VELARDE (architect)
Edward Chambré HARDMAN (photographer)
Church of St Monica, Bootle: interior, 1936
Photograph, 59.3 X 41

Designs for this church are on permanent loan to the British Architectural Library Drawings Collection, RIBA. The sculpture of the reredos is by W. L. Stevenson. The distinctive windows were inspired by the slightly earlier churches of the German architect Dominikus Bohm (1880–1955).

Ref. *A & BN*, 15 January 1937, pp. 70–73.

The E. Chambré Hardman Trust

119.
Bernard Alexander MILLER, 1894–1960
Candlestick, St Christopher's church, Withington, Manchester, 1935
Painted wood, 148 X 47

St Christopher's was demolished in 1994 but its impressive furnishings have been preserved, including the primitivist stone font by Alan Durst (1883–1970) and the Byzantine-style reredos by Mary Adshead (both artists collaborated with Miller on other buildings: St Columba's, Anfield; Holy Cross, Woodchurch, Birkenhead). The candlesticks, by contrast, echo the modern architecture of the church.

The Parish of St Christopher, Withington

Fig. 70 (Cat. 121)

120.
Bernard Alexander MILLER
Candlestick, St Columba's church, Anfield, Liverpool
Painted wood

Probably made by the Liverpool cabinetmaker William Burden.

Refs. *Arch. Rev.*, December 1932, pp. 276–79; *A & BN*, 23 February 1934, pp. 248–52.

St Columba, Anfield

121. (Fig. 70)
Charles Anthony MINOPRIO and
Hugh Greville SPENCELY (architects)
Herbert Raymond MYERSCOUGH-WALKER, 1908–84 (perspectivist)
'Fairacres', Roehampton Lane, London, 1936
Watercolour, 96 X 129

The sixty-four luxury flats in this block range in size from three to four bedrooms with accommodation for servants.

Ref. *A & BN*, 15 January 1937, pp. 90–93.

British Architectural Library Drawings Collection / Royal Institute of British Architects

122.
Herbert J. ROWSE
Philharmonic Hall, Hope Street, Liverpool, 1936–39
Photographs, 23.6 X 29.1 and 28.9 X 23.5

The old Philharmonic Hall of 1846–49, designed by John Cunningham, was destroyed by fire on 5 July 1933. Rowse's plans for rebuilding it on the same site were approved by the Proprietors of the Philharmonic Society on 17 June 1936, and the new building opened on 19 June 1939. Cunningham's classical design was replaced by a block composed for the most part of starkly cubic shapes, comparable to the contemporary work of W. M. Dudok in Holland.

In his final year at the Liverpool School of Architecture, 1932–33, Alwyn Edward Rice chose as the subject of his thesis the design of a new concert hall for Liverpool on a site in Commutation Row. The exhibition of his drawings coincided with the burning of the old Philharmonic Hall, and his scheme therefore attracted special attention and was published in the local press (*Liverpool Post and Mercury*, 11 July 1933). Rice subsequently worked for Rowse on the building of the

Fig. 71 (Cat. 123)

new Philharmonic Hall and the executed design is markedly similar to his thesis, both in the massing of the exterior and the arrangement of the auditorium.

The Board of Trustees of the National Museums & Galleries on Merseyside: Stewart Bale Collection

123. (Fig. 71)
Edmund C. THOMPSON
Design for decoration of the Philharmonic Hall: Apollo Playing to the Animals, 1938/39
Pencil, 50 X 25.5

A design for one of the two gilded reliefs at either end of the upper foyer.

The artist's daughter

124.
Harold DOD, 1890–1965
Harold Cohen Library, University of Liverpool, 1936–38
Photographs

The Harold Cohen Library stands on the site of 'Reilly's Cowshed'. The building illustrates the dilemma of a middle-aged architect in the 1930s, trained in the classical tradition but faced with the new stylistic options of the Modern Movement. The front elevation of Portland stone is a thoroughly classical composition, but stripped of explicitly historical details. By contrast, the book-stack block at the rear is a frankly functional structure of brick and concrete with windows arranged in continuous horizontal bands. Dod, accompanied by Lionel Budden, visited modern continental libraries while preparing his design (*SIS*, pp. 176–77). The sculpture above the main entrance is by Eric Kennington.

The Board of Trustees of the National Museums & Galleries on Merseyside: Stewart Bale Collection

125.
Charles Herbert REILLY
Typescript of radio broadcasts
Book, 26 X 21

Reilly wrote copiously on contemporary architecture for the professional press, but also for lay readers in local and national newspapers (*SIS*, pp. 237–40). Radio

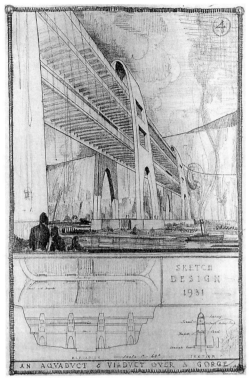

Fig. 72 (Cat. 126)

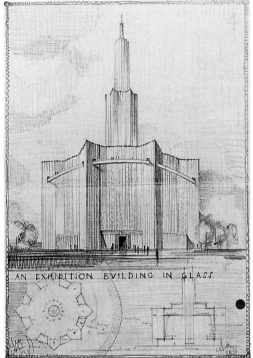

Fig. 73 (Cat. 127)

Fig. 74 (Cat. 129) (Avery Architectural and Fine Arts Library, Columbia University in the City of New York)

broadcasts offered him the opportunity of reaching a wider popular audience. These scripts have titles such as 'The Office Block', 'The Church of Today', 'Architecture and the Public', and 'The New London'. One is dated 25 February 1927, the others are undated.

University Archives, University of Liverpool

126. (Fig. 72)
Alwyn Sheppard FIDLER
Six Hour Sketch: An Aqueduct and Viaduct over a Gorge, 1931
Pencil, 102 X 69

This design for a combined road, rail and canal bridge over a river is also an expression of confidence in the exciting possibilities of reinforced concrete construction.

British Architectural Library Drawings Collection / Royal Institute of British Architects

127. (Fig. 73)
Alwyn Sheppard FIDLER
Six Hour Sketch: An Exhibition Building in Glass, 1931
Pencil, 94.5 X 74

Fidler was obviously aware of the visionary designs for glass buildings by contemporary European modernists. In 1933 he won the RIBA's Victory Scholarship with a design for 'The Buildings and Layout of a Botanical Garden' (*JRIBA*, 28 January 1933, p. 213). His winning scheme was centred on an octagonal glass house which closely resembles this sketch of two years earlier.

British Architectural Library Drawings Collection / Royal Institute of British Architects

128.
Norman Sykes LUNN
Six Hour Sketch: A Domestic Tower in Concrete, 1930
Pencil and watercolour, 91 X 58

The strange sheltering structure over the flat roof is perhaps an echo of Amyas Connel's pioneering modern house, High and Over (published in *A & BN*, 3 January 1930, pp. 12–13).

By kind permission of Mrs N. S. Lunn

129. (Fig. 74)
Edwin Maxwell FRY
City of the Future, 1931
Photograph of an illustration in 'Creative Art', August 1931

One of a series of illustrations of the development of New York published in the 1931 *Regional Plan of New York and its Environs, Vol 2: The Building of the City*, p. 152 (information supplied by Carol Willis). It is not clear why Fry, a young and still relatively unknown architect in England, should have been commissioned to make this drawing. As a student he had spent the summer vacation of his fourth year in the New York office of Carrere and Hastings and it was perhaps through contacts made then that he received the commission. The 'City of Towers' was by this date part of the common currency of modernist architects.

Refs. Jean-Louis Cohen, *Scenes of the World to Come—European Architecture and the American Challenge, 1893–1960*, 1995, pp. 105–06; Robert Stern, Gregory Gilmartin and Thomas Mellins, *New York 1930—Architecture and Urbanism between the two World Wars*, New York, 1987, pp. 441, 646 and 763.

Avery Architectural and Fine Arts Library, Columbia University in the City of New York

130.
Gordon STEPHENSON
Design for a Silk Factory, 1932
Print, 79.8 X 82.8

This was Stephenson's winning entry for the Liverpool Architectural Society's 1932 H. W. Williams Scholarship, an award established in 1930 by a Merseyside cement manufacturer 'for the promotion of the study of architectural design in concrete' (*BLSA*, p. 54). The design was influenced by Le Corbusier, with whom Stephenson had worked in Paris in 1931–32, and also by van den Broek and Owen Williams (letter, Walker Art Gallery files, 29 December 1995).

University of Liverpool Art Gallery and Collections

131. (Fig. 75)
George CHECKLEY, 1893–1960
Thurso, Conduit Head Road, Cambridge, 1932
Photograph

One of a cluster of modernist houses built for Cambridge dons around Conduit Head Road in the early 1930s. Checkley, who was a lecturer in the Cambridge University School of Architecture from 1925, designed White House for himself in 1930–31, followed the next year by Thurso for Professor Hamilton McCombie. Both houses are of concrete frame and rendered brick construction.

Refs. Jeremy Gould, *Modern Houses in Britain, 1919–1939*, 1977, p. 38; *A & BN*, 17 February 1933, pp. 226–29

British Architectural Library Photographs Collection / Royal Institute of British Architects

132.
Charles Herbert REILLY,
Lionel BUDDEN and
J.E. MARSHALL
New building for Liverpool School of Architecture, Abercromby Square, Liverpool: the 'Leverhulme Building', 1933
Photograph, 23.7 X 29

A purpose built home for the School was at last achieved in the year of Reilly's retirement, with funds bequeathed by the first Lord Leverhulme and supplemented by his son. Substantially altered in the 1980s, it consisted originally of a block of studios and teaching rooms arranged around a courtyard attached to the back of four Georgian houses. In scale and choice of materials the 1933 work defers to the old while being recognisably modern, an instance of that 'modernism with ancestry' which Stanley Ramsey praised as the distinctive style of Liverpool architecture students in the early 1930s (*BLSA*, p. 28). It was planned that a Greek Doric column from the recently demolished chapel of the School for the Blind (see cat. 109) should stand in the courtyard 'as a symbol of architecture and of permanent architectural values'.

Ref. *BLSA*, pp. 67 ff.

The Board of Trustees of the National Museums & Galleries on Merseyside: Stewart Bale Collection

Fig. 75 (Cat. 131)

133.
Edwin Maxwell FRY
Miramonte, Coombe, nr. Kingston-on-Thames, 1936–37
Photograph

Miramonte has all the ingredients of the modern house, as preached by continental European architects of the 1920s and 1930s such as Le Corbusier and Mies van der Rohe: flat roofs, sun terraces, horizontal windows, and white-painted concrete walls. For some years after graduating from Liverpool, Fry had worked in the Georgian style at which he had excelled as a student (e.g. Ridge End, Wentworth, Virginia Water, reproduced in *BLSA*, Plate CX). His conversion to modernism seems to date from the early 1930s. Miramonte was commissioned by a former bookmaker and property developer, very different from the intellectuals and aesthetes who were the typical patrons of the modern movement (see Lionel Esher, *A Broken Wave—The Rebuilding of England 1940–1980*, 1981, p. 301).

British Architectural Library Photographs Collection / Royal Institute of British Architects

134. (Fig. 7)
William CRABTREE 1905–91, with
Charles Herbert REILLY and
John Alan SLATER, 1885–1963 and
Arthur Hamilton MOBERLY 1885–1952
Peter Jones department store, Sloane Square, London, 1935–39
Photograph

For his final year thesis as a student at Liverpool, Crabtree designed 'A Departmental Store in Oxford Street' (*A & BN*, 26 July 1929, pp. 114–15). Reilly sent photographs of this scheme—a distinctly Art Deco design with traditional masonry walls—to his friend Spedan Lewis, Chairman of the John Lewis Partnership, who in January 1930 gave Crabtree a job 'doing research work in connection with a rebuilding of the Peter Jones site in Sloane Square' (William Crabtree, autobiographical notes, Walker Art Gallery). This research entailed a visit to Holland and Germany where Crabtree saw buildings by Erich Mendelsohn (1887–1953) including the Columbus House of 1921–31 in Berlin, the influence of which is apparent in the Sloane Square building (*William Crabtree Retrospective*, exhibition catalogue, Guildhall, Guildford, 1992). When the rebuilding scheme was revived after a delay caused by the onset of the Depression, a design team was formed: according to Crabtree, 'the Chairman invited Slater and Moberly, a firm of architects which had recently built a large store for Bourne and Hollingsworth, to join with Reilly and myself in designing and building Peter Jones. Reilly and I were to be responsible for design and appearance, and Slater and Moberly for the

ELEVATION TO OXFORD STREET

Fig. 76 (Cat. 135)

Fig. 77 (Cat. 136)

working drawings and contractual matters. Of course there was some friction as we were all opinionated people, and rival schemes were argued over at the building committee. Reilly did the talking on our side whilst I produced the drawings, and I think we persuaded Slater and Moberly that we were not such crackpots as they first thought. What soon became evident was that in the early 1930s money was just not available for the heavy masonry kind of buildings prevalent and that modern steel buildings demanded a different approach' (autobiographical notes). Economy was one of Spedan Lewis's main requirements of the new building, but he also asked that it should have maximum window space, ease of circulation, high levels of daylight, and be capable of internal rearrangement to accommodate changing trends in shopping (*The Gazette of the John Lewis Partnership*, 13 April 1935, quoted by Jane Bhoyroo). Put up in stages between 1936 and 1939, the building is of concrete-encased steel with a curtain wall of steel and glass (see *Building*, July 1936, pp. 278–83). Reilly modestly took little credit for the design— 'The real author of it is my dear old student William Crabtree. I stand behind agreeing and approving and making an occasional suggestion' (*SIS*, p. 287)—but according to Crabtree 'that the building turned out as well as it did was remarkable and in great measure due to Reilly's enthusiasm and pertinacity. The architectural climate of the day may be recalled by the fact that when I submitted my carefully made elevational drawings and a perspective to the Royal Academy these were duly rejected' (letter to *The Observer*, written 13 March 1959, now with the Lady Reilly). A specific detail of the design which Crabtree credited to Reilly was the use of light-reflecting curved ceilings to the shop windows (David Dean, *The Thirties: Recalling the English Architectural Scene*, 1983, p. 97).

Refs. *The Times*, 31 October 1936; Jane Bhoyroo, *The Rebuilding of the Peter Jones Department Store by William Crabtree*, unpublished BA dissertation, University of Newcastle upon Tyne, 1995.

British Architectural Library Photographs Collection / Royal Institute of British Architects

135. (Fig. 76)
William CRABTREE and
Franz SINGER
Proposed façade for John Lewis department store, Oxford Street, London, c.1937
Pencil and watercolour, 70 X 83

Franz Singer, a Viennese immigrant, joined Crabtree and his design team to work on the rebuilding of the John Lewis Partnership's Oxford Street store (William Crabtree, autobiographical notes).

British Architectural Library Drawings Collection / Royal Institute of British Architects

136. (Fig. 77)
William CRABTREE and
Charles Herbert REILLY (architects)
Raymond Myerscough WALKER (perspectivist)
Proposed John Lewis department store, Oxford Street: perspective of Cavendish Square front, 1937
Ink, pencil and watercolour, 66 X 95

This part of the store was built to A. H. Moberly's alternative design since the ground landlord, Howard de Walden, preferred his scheme to Crabtree's 'glassy bay-windowed proposal' (William Crabtree, autobiographical notes).

British Architectural Library Drawings Collection / Royal Institute of British Architects

137.
Charles Herbert REILLY
Scaffolding in the Sky, 1938
Book

Reilly's autobiography was written five years after his retirement from Liverpool. The choice of the Peter Jones store for the dust jacket illustration underlines the modernist sympathies of the author by this date. For contemporary reactions to the book see: Sheila Turner and Adrian Allan, 'The Papers of Sir Charles Reilly: A Recent Accession to the University Archives', *University of Liverpool Recorder*, no. 81, October 1979, p. 160.

The Lady Reilly

138.
Albert Clifford HOLLIDAY and
Robert Pearce Steel HUBBARD, 1910–65
Barclays Bank, Haifa, c.1935
Photograph, 45.5 X 60

In 1930 Holliday had designed the Jerusalem branch of Barclays Bank with mildly historicist details appropriate to its setting. The Bank's branch in Haifa, designed in partnership with the modernist Liverpool graduate Pearce Hubbard, is more starkly cubic. It is of concrete, cast in situ and faced in stone. The central space inside rises to the full height of the building.

John Holliday

139.
Albert Clifford HOLLIDAY and
Robert Pearce Steel HUBBARD
Shops and apartments, Kingsway, Haifa, 1937
Photograph, 45 X 63

In 1935 Holliday and Hubbard produced a model of this scheme for the rebuilding of part of central Haifa. In execution the blocks were reduced from six storeys to four. Photographs of the buildings were shown in the display of work by past Liverpool students held at the Royal Institute of British Architects, 30 April–14 May 1937, where Reilly considered them the outstanding feature of the exhibition (*SIS*, p. 210).

John Holliday

140. (Cf. Fig. 78)
Christian BARMAN, 1898–1980
HMV Controlled Heat Iron, c.1936
Ceramic, metal, 11.5 X 22.6 X 10.9

This was the first thermostatically controlled electric iron to be successful in Britain, and its innovative technology was matched by its novel appearance, the body and handle being formed in one piece and moulded to fit the hand comfortably. A thumb rest on each side makes the iron suitable for either left or right handed users. This practical, functional product exemplifies Barman's admiration for 'the tradition of straightforward, honest, reticent design . . . nothing but sound sense and absolutely first class taste applied to the problem before you. Not a style, in other words, but *style* pure and simple' (*Arch. Rev.*, July 1933, p. 13).

Cafe Pop/Design Goes Pop

Fig. 78 Advertisement for the HMV Controlled Heat Iron, designed by
Christian Barman, from the catalogue of the Everyday Things exhibition
arranged by the RIBA, 1936. Cf. Cat. 140

141.
Christian BARMAN
HMV Electric fan heater, c.1935
Chrome plated metal, 25.5 X 43 X 26

Instead of imitating the appearance of traditional solid fuel fires Barman's design is based on practical considerations: the curved front spreads heat widely and is free of sharp corners. 'I simply refuse to believe', wrote Barman, 'that it is necessary for electricity to masquerade as coal, gas or candles, or to gate crash into our houses cleverly disguised as these' (*Arch. Rev.*, October 1933, p. 186).

Cafe Pop/Design Goes Pop

142 and 143. (Figs. 79 and 80)
John Henry FORSHAW
Pithead Baths, Treharris, Glamorgan: plans and elevations, 1932
Dyeline prints with colour, 59.2 X 81 and 59.4 X 82

J. H. Forshaw was appointed Chief Architect to the Miners' Welfare Committee in 1926. With six assistant architects he was responsible for providing buildings and recreational facilities catering for the health, social welfare and leisure of the mining communities in England, Scotland and Wales. The construction of pithead baths was the Committee's most conspicuous achievement. These buildings improved on earlier continental examples by completely separating clean and dirty areas and by introducing new, specially designed lockers for storing and drying the miners' clothes. Great emphasis was placed on the standardisation and mass production of components, and the architects worked with a missionary zeal for social improvement (see J. H. Forshaw, 'The Architectural Work of the Miners' Welfare Committee', *JRIBA*, 7 March 1938, pp. 421–38). The better-known pithead baths built under Forshaw—e.g. at Betteshanger Colliery, Kent—are in a conspicuously modern style, asymmetrical and austerely cubic, but the Treharris drawings show that the new facilities could be accommodated behind more traditional elevations. (Treharris was the site of an important early pithead bath building designed by T. E. Richards; see A & BJ, 2 August 1916, pp. 54–55). In 1935 Reilly, proposing Forshaw for admission as a Fellow of the RIBA, wrote: 'I consider the range of great Pithead Baths which have been erected under Mr. Forshaw's direction, some twenty of them or more, one of the big architectural achievements of the present age, as they are one of its greatest social ones. Buildings which might well have been degraded or at best uninteresting have been given by him great simplicity, strength and character'(Forshaw biographical file, RIBA Library).

Glamorgan Record Office, Cardiff

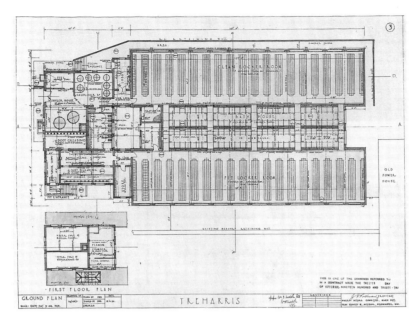

Fig. 79 (Cat. 142) National Monuments Record for Wales

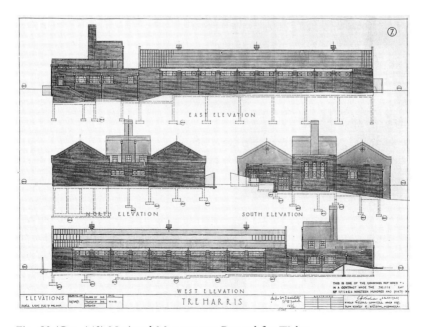

Fig. 80 (Cat. 143) National Monuments Record for Wales

144. (Fig. 81)
John HUGHES, 1903–77
St Andrew's Gardens, Liverpool, 1934–35
Photograph of a watercolour perspective by D. P. Reay, 1935

In August 1931 the recently graduated John Hughes was taken on as an assistant by Liverpool's Director of Housing, Lancelot Keay. Hughes's first design was for a semicircular block of flats in Regent Road which remained unbuilt, but he used the same form in the north block of St Andrew's Gardens, completed in 1935. The model for this was the so-called Horseshoe Estate at Britz, designed by Bruno Taut and Martin Wagner, which Keay had admired on a fact-finding visit to Berlin in June 1931 (Frank Newberry, *Flats in Liverpool, 1919–1939*, B.Arch. thesis, Liverpool School of Architecture, 1981). Walter Gropius visited St Andrew's Gardens, expressing admiration for the horizontal emphasis of the windows but remarking, ominously, that higher tower blocks with more open space around them would have been better (*Liverpool Daily Post*, 19 May 1934, p. 6). George Orwell had misgivings about the social impact of such flats rather than their architectural quality: 'the blocks of workers' flats in the centre of [Liverpool], modelled I believe, on the workers' flats in Vienna, are definitely fine buildings. But there is something ruthless and soulless about the whole business' (George Orwell, *The Road to Wigan Pier*, 1937, p. 71). Only part of the scheme shown in Cat. 144 was carried out.

City of Liverpool Libraries and Information Services: Liverpool Record Office

145. (Fig. 82)
Alwyn Sheppard FIDLER
Axonometric view of hostel group, c.1936
Pencil, 101 X 91.5

This drawing seems to show a scheme for student housing on a site bounded by Ashton Street, Brownlow Hill and Crown Street. The Harold Cohen Library (1936–38) is shown much as built, suggesting that the drawing was made while Fidler was studying in the Department of Civic Design, after graduating B.Arch. in 1932. The accommodation blocks, with their sweeping curves and rounded projecting stair towers, show the influence of continental housing schemes and closely resemble St Andrew's Gardens, built further down Brownlow Hill in 1934–35 (see cat. 144)

British Architectural Library Drawings Collection / Royal Institute of British Architects

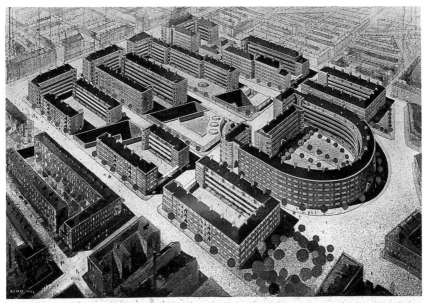

CITY OF LIVERPOOL HOUSING · ST. ANDREWS GARDENS

Fig. 81 (Cat. 144)

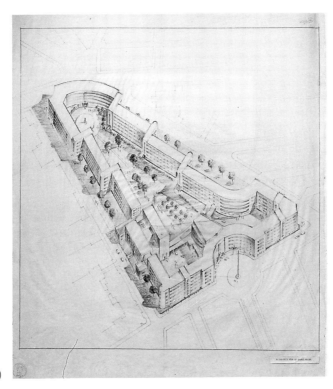

Fig. 82 (Cat. 145)

146. (Fig. 83)
William HOLFORD and
Gordon STEPHENSON (designers)
William BURDEN, maker
Table lamp, 1933
Chrome on brass, stainless steel and rosewood, 75 X 27

Presented to Reilly by his colleagues on his retirement. The lamp is a model of a traffic pylon designed by Holford and Stephenson for a site at the bottom of Bold Street, Liverpool, for the Railway Centenary celebrations of 1930.

Refs. *BLSA*, plate LX; *Arch. Rev.* September 1933, p. 118.

John Sheppard Fidler

147. (Fig. 84)
Augustus JOHN 1878–1961
Portrait of Charles Reilly, 1931
Oil on canvas, 49 X 39

John taught at the Art Sheds from 1901–03 and was still in Liverpool when Reilly arrived in 1904 (*SIS*, pp. 86–89). He painted a number of portraits for the University Club (*Art Sheds*, cat. nos. 82–85) and it is not surprising that Reilly should have wanted John to paint his own commemorative portrait when the University decided to commission one (*SIS*, p. 318). John wrote to Reilly on 15 May 1931, saying that he would be proud to undertake this, and in August invited Reilly to stay at his house, Fryern Court, Fordingbridge (LUA, D207/40/53 and 54). Reilly wrote to his wife from Fryern on 7, 8 and 9 September, describing work on the portrait then in progress (D207/37/1–3). According to the account in Reilly's autobiography, he sat to John each day from ten until one and again from two-thirty to five-thirty, 'by which time I, at any rate, was nearly dead. He seemed to look into my soul in such a searching way that I wilted under it . . . I think he painted me three times, but I only saw the last and that just as I was leaving. I hope the other two canvases appear some day in galleries as portraits of a tramp or something of the sort. I should be glad if I had been a useful model to make up for his kindness in painting me at all' (*SIS*, p. 319). John seems to have planned to make finishing touches to the portrait in December 1931 (D207/40/55).

While he was staying with John, Reilly wrote to his wife: 'I have suggested his building a large new studio, modern, in ferro concrete, and he likes the idea' (D207/37/3). Reilly seems thus to have helped bring about the remarkable studio

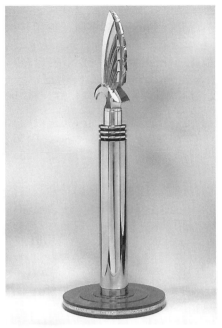

Fig. 83 (Cat. 146)   Fig. 84 (Cat. 147)

which Christopher Nicholson built at Fryern in 1933–34; John wrote to Reilly enthusiastically about it soon after it was completed (D207/40/56).

University of Liverpool Art Gallery and Collections

148. (Front cover)
Edward Chambré HARDMAN
Portrait of Charles Reilly, 1924
Photograph, 43 X 36.2

The Board of Trustees of the National Museums & Galleries on Merseyside: Walker Art Gallery

149.
Charles Herbert REILLY and Naim ASLAN, b.1910
***An Outline Plan for the County Borough of Birkenhead*, 1947**
Book, 31.2 X 25

After his retirement Reilly became increasingly interested in issues of town planning and social housing. He pushed the idea of arranging houses in neighbourly groups with their front doors facing the street and their back doors giving access to a common green or playground. The idea became known as the 'Reilly Green' and was introduced on a grand scale into this replanning scheme for Birkenhead, begun during the Second World War, which Reilly produced with one of his former students. The 'Reilly Green' arrangement was not carried out at Birkenhead but examples were built at Dudley and Bilston in the West Midlands. See Lawrence Wolfe, *The Reilly Plan, A New Way of Life*, 1945.

Edward Morris

150.
Album of press cuttings relating to the Birkenhead Plan, with a caricature of Charles Reilly by Marjorie Holford, 1944
32.5 X 24.7

The polygonal 'Reilly Greens' are shown in the background of this caricature by Marjorie Holford, wife of W. G. Holford.

University Archives, University of Liverpool

151.
Charles Reilly's walking stick
Wood and ivory, 90 X 5

The Lady Reilly

152.
Lionel BUDDEN (editor)
***The Book of the Liverpool School of Architecture*, 1932**

Reilly described this publication as follows: 'A big volume Budden had largely written, edited and published, on the work of the School . . . It contains photographs of buildings by old students in all parts of the world and the best of the School drawings to date. It was given me at the opening of the School Exhibition in July 1932, though it was designed to mark the completion of my twenty-fifth year at the School, which took place in 1929. The intervening years were taken up preparing it. That shows the trouble to which Budden went. The old students in 1929 wanted to have my portrait painted but I thought such a record would be more useful to the School' (*SIS*, p. 312). The book is a fitting climax to the sequence of publications of his students' works which Reilly had begun in 1906 with the Portfolio of Measured Drawings (cat. 25 and 26). The list of subscribers printed at the front is a roll call of distinguished former students and professional colleagues in Britain and overseas.

Edward Morris

153.
Lawrence WRIGHT
The Life and Career of Archie Teck, 1930s
Film

This animated cartoon charts the progress of a young graduate of Reilly's School from early disappointment to eventual triumph. In search of his first job, he takes his portfolio to a succession of architects but in each case manages to show an inappropriate drawing: the Gothic Revivalists laugh at his International Style office block, the flashy modernist dismisses his study of the Ionic order, and his six hour sketch of 'A Group of Cathedrals on a Rocky Island' excites no admiration. After a comically unsuccessful suicide attempt he enters and wins a competition for a major civic building, and his future success is assured. He rises steadily through the profession, ending up as 'Teck, R. A.', and is last seen turning away a hopeful job applicant, another new graduate with a letter of recommendation from Reilly.

Piano accompaniment recorded by Robert Orledge, 1 April 1996.

Video recording supplied by the National Film and Television Archive of the British Film Institute; shown by permission of the Wright Family

Biographies of
Liverpool-trained Architects
Represented in the Exhibition

ADAMS, William Naseby c.1887–1952

Son of Vicar of St Augustine's, Everton. Attended Liverpool College. Won first prize in competition to design a block of cottages at Port Sunlight, 1905. Dip. Arch. 1908. Worked on Merseyside for Briggs, Wolstenholme, Hobbs & Thornely, then in partnership with Duncan Campbell. Settled in London after First World War. Chief Assistant to Lutyens on Britannic House. Won Dewsbury War Memorial competition with Eric Ross Arthur (q.v.), 1923. Designed houses in Guildford and Gerrard's Cross. Chief Assistant to Berry Webber on Peterborough Town Hall and Southampton Civic Centre. Active on various RIBA committees.

Refs: Obituary, *JRIBA*, September 1952, p. 425; student record card.

ALLEN, Joseph Stanley b.1898

Attended Liverpool Collegiate School. Entered Liverpool School of Architecture 1915. B. Arch. 1922. After two years in Philadelphia and New York, including work on Hotel Roosevelt, New York, for George B. Post & Sons and New York Cotton Exchange for Donn Barber, returned to Liverpool to work with H. J. Rowse on India Buildings, 1924–28. Lecturer in Architecture, University of Liverpool from 1930. Appointed Head of Leeds School of Architecture 1933. Designed modernist Post Office, Parkgate, Wirral, 1935. Appointed Professor of Town and Country Planning, Durham University, 1945.

Refs: British Architectural Library, RIBA, biography file; student record card.

ARTHUR, Eric Ross 1898–1981

Born Dunedin, New Zealand, and trained there under the Arts and Crafts architect Basil Hooper. War service, 1917–18. Kitchener Scholar, Liverpool University

1919, B. Arch. 1922. Worked for Lutyens and Sir Aston Webb. Won Dewsbury War Memorial competition with W. N. Adams (q.v.), 1923; appointed Professor of Architecture at Toronto University later the same year. Worked extensively in the fields of Canadian architectural history and conservation.

Refs: Information from Michael Findlay, Otago Early Settlers Museum, Dunedin; student record card. Eric Ross Arthur's papers are held by the Metro Toronto Reference Library

ASLAN, Naim b.1910

With the Public Works Department, Baghdad, 1930–31. Entered Liverpool School of Architecture 1932. Working in London with P. D. Hepworth, 1938. Collaborated with Reilly on *An Outline Plan for the County Borough of Birkenhead*, published 1947.

Ref: student record card.

BARMAN, Christian 1898–1980

Son of a Scandinavian merchant seaman. Family moved to Wirral following outbreak of First World War. Cert. Arch. 1918. Worked briefly for Lutyens. Founder of *Architecture* (journal of the Society of Architects), and editor November 1922–April 1925; editor of the *Architectural Review*, 1927–33, and the *Architect's Journal*. Published *The Danger to St Pauls*, 1925, and *Balbus*, c.1926. Work as a freelance industrial designer includes innovative designs for the household appliance department of HMV in the 1930s. Architectural work includes Oratory Central Schools, Chelsea, and Kinara, Esher Place, Surrey, for Hugh Quigley (*Arch. Rev.*, April 1935). Publicity Officer to London Passenger Transport Board, 1935–41. Assistant Director of Postwar Building, Ministry of Works, 1941–45, Public Relations adviser to GWR, 1945–47, Chief Publicity Officer to British Transport Commission, 1947–62.

Refs: Bruce Paget, *An Evaluation of the Work of Christian Barman OBE, RDI*, unpublished undergraduate thesis, Trent Polytechnic, 1988, available in London Transport Museum library; Christian Barman, *The Man Who Built London Transport*, 1979; obituary, *The Times*, 11 October 1980; student record card.

BARNISH, Leonard 1885–1975

Cert. Arch. 1903. In partnership with George Hastwell Grayson, 1912–33. President of Liverpool Architectural Society, 1933. Works include housing at Bebington, Wirral, and, with Grayson, Southport War Memorial. Collaborated with Herbert Thearle (q.v.) and Herbert Silcock on design of Liverpool Orphanage (1939 RIBA Bronze Medal for Building of Merit).

Refs. Obituary, *Building*, 21 February 1975, p. 63; student record card.

BRADSHAW, Donald 1900–71

Attended council school. At Liverpool School of Architecture 1920–21. Joined office of H.J. Rowse (q.v.), 1922, working on most of the office's principal commissions. According to J. S. Allen (q.v., a contemporary in Rowse's office), Bradshaw was responsible for the 'exquisite detailing' of these buildings. Set up in independent practice in 1952, working on high rise housing and schools, locally and nationally. In 1965, after Rowse's death, became senior partner in Bradshaw, Rowse and Harker Associates.

Refs: Information from Michael Shippobottom; student record card.

BRADSHAW, Harold Chalton 1893–1943

Attended Holt Secondary School, Liverpool. 1908 entered Liverpool School of Architecture as 'lantern and studio boy', enrolling as a student 1911. Cert. Arch. 1913. First Rome Scholar, 1913; scholarship interrupted by war service. First Secretary of Royal Fine Art Commission, 1923. Lecturer in History of Architecture, Architectural Association. Published report on the architecture of the 1925 Paris Exhibition. Buildings include: Guards' Memorial, London; Memorial to the Missing, Ploegsteert Wood, Belgium; French House, Lympne, Kent; Burningfold Farm, Dunsfold, Surrey; branches of Lloyds Bank at Caterham-on-the-Hill and Caversham.

Refs: student record card.

BRIDGWATER, Derek Lawley 1899–1983

Attended Solihull School. Entered Liverpool School of Architecture 1920, B. Arch 1924, lecturer and studio instructor 1926–30. Became Reilly's son-in-law 1930. Buildings include Frances Gray House, Stepney; branches of Barclays Bank at Horley and Sevenoaks; St Felix's School, Southwold; St Swithun's School, Winchester; RC Chapel, Hammersmith; North Gate flats, Regents Park, London.

Refs: student record card.

BUDDEN, Lionel Bailey 1887–1956

Attended Merchant Taylors' School, Crosby. Entered Liverpool School of Architecture 1905, BA 1909, MA 1910. Began teaching at the School in 1911, acted as Reilly's second-in-command becoming Associate Professor in 1924, and succeeded him as Roscoe Professor in 1933. Retired 1952. RIBA Essay Medal 1923. Buildings include: War memorials in Birkenhead and Liverpool; Liverpool veterinary hospital; extensions to Liverpool University Students' Union; new building for Liverpool School of Architecture, Abercromby Square; William Henry Cocker Memorial Tower, Stanley Park, Blackpool. Won competition for additions to Kings College, Cambridge, in partnership with Herbert Rowse (*Builder*, 9 November 1923); not carried out.

Refs: Obituary, *JRIBA*, September 1956, p. 478; student record card.

CHECKLEY, George 1893–1960

Born New Zealand. Trained for a year under the Christchurch architect Cecil Wood before serving for three years in the New Zealand Expeditionary Forces. Attended Liverpool School of Architecture 1919–22 on ex-serviceman's grant. Awarded Henry Jarvis Studentship tenable at the British School at Rome, 1922. Lecturer at Cambridge University School of Architecture from 1925. Master of Regent Street Polytechnic School of Architecture from 1934. Head of Nottingham University School of Architecture 1937–48. Buildings: White House, 1930–31, and Thurso, 1932, both Cambridge.

Refs: Obituary by Stephen Welsh (q.v.) *JRIBA*, January 1961, p. 105; Jeremy Gould, *Modern Houses in Britain 1919–1939*, 1977; British School at Rome, Jarvis Student files; information from Michael Findlay and Alan Powers; student record card.

CRABTREE, William 1905–91

Attended Doncaster Grammar School. Worked for the Doncaster practice of T. H. Johnson before coming to study at the Liverpool School of Architecture on the advice of Patrick Abercrombie, an associate of his father. Spent the summer of 1928 in the New York office of Harvey Wiley Corbett. RIBA Tite Prize, 1928. Dip. Arch. 1929. Worked as a perspectivist for Joseph Emberton, 1929. Employed by the John Lewis Partnership, 1930–c.1939, working on the design of its stores in Sloane Square and Oxford Street, London. Taught at the Architectural Association in the mid-1930s. Member of MARS. Involved in post-war replanning and rebuilding of Southampton and Plymouth, and in the design of housing for New Towns at Crawley, Hatfield and Harlow.

Refs: Autobiographical notes, Walker Art Gallery files; Obituary, *The Times*, 12 March 1991; *William Crabtree Retrospective*, exhibition catalogue, Guidhall, Guildford, 16–21 May 1992; student record card.

DAVIES, Harold Hinchliffe d.1960

Attended Liverpool College. Studied at Liverpool School of Architecture 1919–20. In 1925 entered into practice with his father, Harold Edward Davies (d.1952), a specialist in the design of public houses. Designed numerous licensed premises on Merseyside, including: The Blackburne Arms, Catharine Street; The Clock Inn, London Road; The Clubmoor Hotel; The Gardeners' Arms, Broad Green; and The Jolly Miller, West Derby. Rebuilt the Liverpool Corn Exchange, Fenwick Street, after destruction in Second World War.

Refs: Stewart Bale client index, NMGM Archives; Obituary, *JRIBA*, November 1960; student record card.

DOD, Harold Alfred 1890–1965

Attended Southport Grammar School. Entered Liverpool School of Architecture 1906; BA 1909, MA 1910. Lecturer and Studio Instructor, 1912–14. Assistant to Reilly on the Students' Union building. Joined the Liverpool practice of Willink and Thicknesse to work on the Cunard Building, 1914. The firm became Willink and Dod in 1920. Liverpool buildings include: offices for Royal Exchange Assurance Company, 1927; The Athenaeum, completed 1928; Derby and Rathbone Halls of Residence, Mossley Hill; and the Harold Cohen Library. Other works include a vestibule for Gibraltar Cathedral; Thor's Hill, Thurstaston, Wirral; and Spillers Dog Biscuit Factory, Birkenhead. Retired 1956.

Refs: Allan Billinge, *A Century of Practice—The Gilling Dod Partnership*, 1981/82; archives of Gilling Dod Partnership; student record card.

DOUGILL, Wesley 1893–1943

Attended Yove Bridge Grammar School. Entered Liverpool School of Architecture 1919; B.Arch. and Cert. Civic Design 1922, MA 1924. RIBA Measured Drawings Medal 1923. First Special Premium, British School at Rome, 1920. Research Fellow, Department of Civic Design, and co-editor of *The Town*

Planning Review from 1926, editor from 1935. Chief Town Planning Assistant, London County Council, 1940. Worked with Abercrombie and Forshaw (q.v.) on County of London Plan.

Refs: Obituaries, *JRIBA*, March 1943, and *AJ*, 25 February 1943, p. 148; student record card.

FIDLER, Alwyn Gwilym Sheppard 1909–90

Attended Holywell County School. Entered Liverpool School of Architecture 1927. Summer 1931 working for Zantzinger, Borie and Medary, Philadelphia, USA. Graduated 1932. RIBA Victory Scholarship and Rome Scholarship, 1933. Office experience with Grey Wornum and Herbert J. Rowse. Appointed Chief Architect to the Land Settlement Association, 1937. Appointed Chief Architect of Crawley New Town, 1947. First City Architect of Birmingham, 1952–64. Civic Trust Awards for Lydhurst Estate and Hawkesley Moat Farm Estate, Birmingham, 1961. Vice President RIBA. Member of the Faculty of Architecture of the British School at Rome.

Refs: Obituaries, *AJ*, 21 February 1990, and *JRIBA*, June 1990, p. 91; student record card.

FORSHAW, John Henry 1895–1973

Attended Ormskirk Grammar School. Articled to Thomas Myddleton Shallcross. Entered Liverpool School of Architecture 1919. Summer 1920 with Flagg & Chambers, New York. B.Arch. 1922, Cert. Civic Design 1924. Worked for Liverpool Corporation 1923–26. Chief Architect, Miners' Welfare Committee, 1926–39. Architect to the London County Council and Superintending Architect of Metropolitan Buildings, 1941–46 (Deputy 1939–41). Prepared 1943 County of London Plan with Patrick Abercrombie. Chief Architect and Housing Consultant, Ministry of Health, 1946–59, and of Ministry of Housing and Local Government, 1951–59.

Refs: Obituary, *Building*, 21 September 1973, p. 92; student record card.

FRY, Edwin Maxwell 1899–1987

Attended Liverpool Institute High School. Entered Liverpool School of Architecture in February 1920. Worked for Carrère & Hastings, New York, summer 1922. B.Arch. 1923. Went to London 1923, worked for Adams & Thompson, and for

Southern Railways as chief architectural designer carrying out additions and alterations to railway stations and hotels in London, Southampton and Ramsgate. Associate Partner with Adams & Thompson from 1927. During early 1930s abandoned neo-Georgian (e.g. Ridge End, Virginia Water, Surrey, 1930) in favour of modernism (e.g. Sassoon House, Peckham, London, 1933–34). In partnership with Walter Gropius, 1936. Founder member of MARS. Post-Second World War work in Africa and India, as well as UK. Royal Gold Medal for Architecture, 1964.

Refs: Maxwell Fry, *Autobiographical Sketches*, 1975; student record card.

GEE, Ernest

Educated in Lausanne. Entered Liverpool School of Architecture 1908, Cert. Arch. 1910, followed by three months in Paris and Rome, measuring buildings. Entered into partnership with Edgar Quiggin. They did much domestic, church, school and commercial work across Merseyside and North Wales, including: Gas Offices and showroom, Bold Street, Liverpool, 1938; hospital block, National Children's Home, Frodsham, 1938; Bishop Chavasse Memorial Church, Norris Green, Liverpool, 1933.

Refs: *Liverpolitan*, January 1938; archives of Parry, Boardman, Morris; student record card.

HARRIS, Philip Capes b.1891

Attended Parkfield School, Liverpool. Entered Liverpool School of Architecture 1908, Cert. Arch. 1910. Entered RA School of Architecture 1910 and worked as assistant to various London architects, including Blow & Billery and Lutyens. Government Architect, Zanzibar, from 1922.

Ref: University Archives, University of Liverpool, photograph album A 152; student record card.

HOLFORD, William Graham 1907–75

Born Johannesburg, South Africa. Entered Liverpool School of Architecture 1925. Office experience with Voorhees, Gmelin & Walker, New York, 1929. B. Arch. 1930. Rome Prize 1930. Appointed Senior Lecturer, Liverpool School of Architecture, 1933. Appointed Lever Professor of Civic Design, University of Liverpool, 1936. 1939–45, supervising construction of ordnance factories and hostels. Professor of Town Planning, University College, London, 1948–70. President

RIBA 1960–62. Royal Gold Medal for Architecture, 1963. Architectural and planning work includes: Team Valley industrial estate, Newcastle upon Tyne; precinct of St Paul's Cathedral, London; University of Kent, Canterbury; Barclay's Bank, Maidstone.

Refs: Gordon E. Cherry and Leith Penny, *Holford, a study in architecture, planning and civic design*, 1986; British School at Rome, Rome Scholar file; student record card.

HOLLIDAY, Albert Clifford 1897–1960

Attended Bradford Grammar School. Entered Liverpool School of Architecture 1915; Dip. Civic Design 1920, B. Arch. 1922. Spent long vacation 1920 at the Ecole des Beaux Arts, Paris. Research Fellow, Department of Civic Design, and joint editor of *The Town Planning Review*, 1921–23. Civic Adviser to the City of Jerusalem, 1922–26. Private practice in Palestine from 1927. Consultant, Ceylon and Gibraltar, 1939–46. Joined Stevenage Development Corporation 1946, becoming Chief Architect and Planner. Appointed Professor of Town and Country Planning, Manchester University, 1952.

Refs: Obituaries, *Builder*, 7 October 1960, p. 660, and *The Times*, 29 September 1960; student record card.

HUBBARD, Robert Pearce Steel 1910–65

Born Glasgow, son of a ship designer. Attended Bedford School. Entered Liverpool School of Architecture 1927. Fourth-year vacation with MacGinnis & Walsh, Boston, Mass., and Shreve, Lamb & Harmon, New York. Graduated 1932. Rome Scholarship, 1932. Gave up Scholarship, went from Rome to Jerusalem, and joined in practice with Clifford Holliday (q.v.), 1934. Married Frances Bruce, Rome Scholar in Sculpture. Was in partnership with Austen St B. Harrison from 1937. Later work includes: replanning scheme for Malta; University of Accra, Ghana; and Queen Elizabeth Hospital, Aden.

Refs. Obituary, *Builder*, 17 September 1965, p. 604; British School at Rome, Rome Scholar file; student record card.

HUGHES, John 1903–77

Attended Llanrwst Secondary School. Entered Liverpool School of Architecture 1926, B. Arch. 1931. Final year thesis design, A Stadium for Liverpool, awarded gold medal at the Olympic Art Exhibition, Los Angeles, 1932. Assistant to Lancelot Keay, Director of Housing, Liverpool City Council, 1931–34. Appointed Deputy Director of Housing, Manchester City Council, 1934. Director of Housing, Manchester City Council, 1938–46. Director of Housing, City of Westminster, 1946–50. Principal architect to the Ministry of Housing and Local Government for Wales from 1950 until retirement in 1963.

Refs: *Liverpool Post*, 14 March 1934; *Municipal Journal*, 3 June 1938; *Manchester Evening News*, 24 June 1946; British Architectural Library, RIBA, biography file; student record card.

KENYON, George 1908–76

Attended Sefton Park Council School. Entered Liverpool School of Architecture 1925. Summer vacation 1928 with Shreve, Lamb & Harmon, New York. Dip.Arch. with Distinction, 1930. Worked for Liverpool Corporation Housing Department, 1930. In Herbert J. Rowse's office, 1932. Architectural Assistant, Leeds Corporation, 1934. City Architect of Newcastle upon Tyne, 1947–73.

Refs: Press cuttings, Newcastle upon Tyne Central Library; student record card.

LAKSMINARASAPPA, Srinivasarao Harti born c.1885

Came to Liverpool with qualifications from the University of Madras and the College of Civil Engineering, Madras. Cert.Arch. 1912, B.Arch 1921. Following return to India became Architectural Executive Engineer in the Mysore Public Works Department; Principal of the College of Engineering, Bangalore; and, by 1933, Government Architect to the Government of Mysore.

Refs: Reilly letter book, University Archives, University of Liverpool, D207/2/3, 25 October 1910; student record card.

LAWRENCE, Frederick Orchard 1893–1971

Attended St Margaret's H.G. School, Liverpool. Entered Liverpool School of Architecture 1910. B.Arch. 1915, following two years in the office of Briggs & Thornely. Rome Scholarship 1920, following war service. Returned from Rome to Briggs & Thornely, worked on competition drawings of Herbert Rowse's design for India Buildings and on the Northern Ireland Parliament Building

(Stormont). With Edmund Kirby & Sons in 1925. In partnership with Colonel Beckwith, Liverpool, 1930.

Ref: British School at Rome, Rome Scholar file; student record card.

LUNN, Norman Sykes 1908–92

Son of a Huddersfield architect. Attended Silcoates School, Wakefield. Entered Liverpool School of Architecture 1926. Spent fourth year summer vacation in New York with Corbett, Harrison & MacMurray. B.Arch. 1931. Practised in Huddersfield.

Ref: student record card.

LYON, Maurice b.1887

Attended Birkenhead School. Entered Liverpool School of Architecture 1903, BA 1906. Made measured drawings of Sanmicheli's buildings in Verona, 1906. Spent several years in H. V. Lanchester's office. Government Architect, Ministry of Works, Cairo, 1920s–1930s. Designed State Telegraphs and Telephones building and Egyptian State Archives building, both Cairo. Following return to Britain, employed by Office of Works.

Refs: University Archives, University of Liverpool, photograph album, A 152; student record card.

MARTIN, Edward William 1891–1977

Born in Scotland, brought up in Delaware, USA. Graduated University of Delaware 1916. Architecture classes at University of Pennsylvania. Office experience with Wilson, Eyre & McIlvanie, Philadelphia, and Sir Percy Scott Worthington, Manchester, England. B.Arch., University of Liverpool, 1922. Returned to USA with J. S. Allen (q.v.) after graduation. Practised in Wilmington, Delaware, until his death. Did much work for Pierre S. Dupont, head of the Dupont Corporation. Buildings include: Banquet Room on the estate of Pierre S. Dupont, near Kennett Square, Pennsylvania, 1928; Delaware State Legislative Building, Dover, 1932; Pierre S. Dupont High School, Wilmington, 1934; US Post Office, Court House and Custom House, Wilmington, 1935.

Refs: E. W. Martin, 'Some differences between English and American architectural office practice', *The Builder*, 25 February 1921, pp. 256–57; archives of the American Institute of Architects, Washington DC; Sandra L. Tatman and Roger

W. Moss, *Biographical Dictionary of Philadelphia Architects 1700–1930*, Boston, 1985; student record card.

MASON, Harold Clayforth 1892–1960

Attended Windermere Grammar School. Trained with his father before entering Liverpool School of Architecture, 1909. Cert.Arch. 1911. Studied at RA while working as assistant to C. H. B. Quennell. RIBA Measured Drawings Medal, 1913. In 1920, after war service in India and Middle East, joined Public Works Department in Iraq as Assistant Government Architect, later Government Architect. Left Iraq 1935 to enter into partnership with James Mollison Wilson, former Director of Public Works in Iraq. Buildings in Baghdad include: Post and Telegram Office, 1929; Villa Harathiyat, 1933; St George's Church; Headquarters of Royal Agricultural Society; Royal College of Medicine.

Refs: Khalid Sultani, 'Architecture in Iraq between the Two World Wars 1920–1940', *International Magazine of Arab Culture*, 2/3, 1982, pp. 93 ff; C. H. Lindsey Smith, *JM—The Story of an Architect*, n/d; obituary, *JRIBA*, March 1960, p. 185; student record card.

MILLER, Bernard Alexander 1894–1960

Cert.Arch. 1914, B.Arch. 1928. Taught at Liverpool School of Architecture for many years from 1919 and practised as a designer of churches and church furnishings. Works include: St Columba's, Anfield; St Aidans's, Speke, St Christopher's, Norris Green; St Christopher's, Withington; screens at St Helen's, Garstang, Lancashire and Holy Cross, Woodchurch, Birkenhead, the latter carved by Alan Durst. Acted as architect to Chester Cathedral, and was responsible for imaginative restoration and rebuilding at St Michael and All Angels, Tettenhall, Staffordshire.

Refs: obituary (by Herbert Thearle, q.v.), *JRIBA* November 1960, p. 22; student record card.

MINOPRIO, Charles Anthony 1900–88

Attended Harrow and University College, Oxford, before entering Liverpool School of Architecture, 1920. Office experience with Thomas Hastings, New York, 1924. B. Arch. 1925, MA 1928. Awarded Henry Jarvis Studentship, tenable at the British School at Rome, 1925. Entered into partnership with Hugh Greville Spencely, 1928, and won competition for Ramsgate Harbour Station site, 1929.

Minoprio & Spencely's 1930s works include: extension to School for the Blind, Liverpool; 'Fairacres', Roehampton Lane, London; 'Broadlands', Ascot, Berkshire, 1932; Vitasan Clinic, Sevenoaks, Kent; the Good Intent restaurant, King's Road, Chelsea (with murals by Edward Halliday); Crawford's warehouse, Willesden, London. After the Second World War the practice worked on planning schemes for Chelmsford, Worcester, Crawley and Cwmbran, and for Kuwait and Baghdad. Minoprio published *The Minor Domestic Architecture of Gloucestershire* in 1931.

Refs: obituaries, *Times*, 5 March 1988, and *Daily Telegraph*, 9 March 1988; British School at Rome, Jarvis Scholar file; family papers; student record card.

PRESTWICH, Ernest 1889–1977

Attended Manchester Grammar School. Entered Liverpool School of Architecture 1906, BA 1910. Won 1910 competition for planning the completion of Port Sunlight. MA 1912. Joined family practice in Leigh, Lancashire and subsequently worked for the architects department of Lever Brothers on projects including the Thornton Hough War Memorial and Stornoway Planning Scheme. Won many architectural competitions: Blackpool War Memorial; Harrogate War Memorial; Doncaster War Memorial; Leigh War Memorial; Knowsley House, Bolton; Midland Bank House, Manchester; Leeds Public Baths; Northampton Police and Fire Station, Sessions Court and Public Baths; and, with Sir Percy Thomas, Swinton and Pendlebury Town Hall.

Refs: information from Michael Shippobottom; student record card.

QUIGGIN, Edgar

Entered Liverpool School of Architecture and Applied Art 1897, Cert. Arch. 1899. Later joined in partnership by Edward Gee (q.v.).

Ref: student record card.

RICE, Alwyn Edward 1909–79

Attended Liverpool Institute. Entered Liverpool School of Architecture 1928, graduated 1933. Worked with Herbert Rowse on the new Philharmonic Hall, Liverpool, completed 1939. During Second World War worked for William Holford (q.v.) on accommodation for munitions factories. Later took over the practice of Quiggin & Gee (q.v.).

Refs: information from family; student record card.

ROWSE, Herbert James 1887–1963

Entered Liverpool School of Architecture 1905, Cert. Arch. 1907. Travelled in Italy 1908 (measured drawings published in *Architectural Engineer*, 4 August 1909). Assistant to Frank Simon on the Manitoba Parliament Buildings, Winnipeg, Canada, 1909–11. Travel and study in America, 1912. After war service commenced practice in Liverpool, 1918. In 1924 won competitions for India Buildings, Liverpool (in partnership with Briggs, Wostenholme & Thornely); Heswall Golf Club House, Wirral; and New Library and Chambers at King's College, Cambridge (with Lionel Budden; not built). Other works include: housing schemes at Whiston, 1924, and Rainhill, 1925 (both Lancashire); Martins Bank head office, Water Street, Liverpool, 1927–32; Lloyd's Bank, Church Street, Liverpool, 1928–32; additions to St Paul's Eye Hospital and Royal Southern Hospital, Liverpool, 1929; headquarters for Compania de Applicaciones Electricas, S.A., Barcelona, Spain, 1930 (not built); flats, Camden Street, Birkenhead; Mersey Tunnel entrances and ventilating towers, 1931–34; Philharmonic Hall, Liverpool, 1936–39; headquarters for Pharmaceutical Society of Great Britain, Brunswick Square, London, 1937; UK Pavilion, Empire Exhibition, Glasgow, 1938; Woodchurch Estate, Birkenhead, 1946.

Refs: J. A. Haddy, *Herbert J. Rowse, Architect of Quality, 1887–1963*, unpublished thesis, 1978, Liverpool Record Office; family papers; archives of Bradshaw, Rowse & Harker; student record card.

SPENCELY, Hugh Greville 1900–83

Attended Harrow and Royal Military Academy, Woolwich, before entering Liverpool School of Architecture in 1921. B. Arch. 1926, Dip. Civic Design 1928. Entered into partnership with Anthony Minoprio, 1928 (see under Minoprio for their joint works).

Refs: autobiographical notes; student record card.

STEPHENSON, Gordon b.1908

Attended Liverpool Institute. Entered Liverpool School of Architecture 1925. In 1929 spent six months in the New York office of Corbett, Harrison & McMurray. B. Arch. 1930. Chadwick Trust Scholarship, 1930, allowing two years study at the Institut d'Urbanisme, University of Paris, and work in the office of Le Corbusier. Taught fourth and fifth year students at Liverpool School of Architecture 1932–36. Held Commonwealth Fellowship at Massachusetts Institute of Technology,

1936–38. Senior Planner with the nascent Ministry of Town and Country Planning during Second World War, followed by work on Stevenage New Town. Lever Professor of Civic Design, University of Liverpool, 1948–53. Has subsequently held chairs at the Universities of Toronto and Western Australia.

Refs: Gordon Stephenson, *On a Human Scale: A Life in City Design*, South Fremantle, 1992; Gordon E. Cherry and Leith Penny, *Holford: a study in architecture, planning and civic design*, 1986; University Archives, University of Liverpool; student record card.

THEARLE, Herbert 1903–71

Attended Oulton Secondary School. Already an articled pupil with Briggs & Thornely when he enrolled at Liverpool School of Architecture in 1920. Worked on Northern Ireland Parliament Building (Stormont) and Barnsley Town Hall. Holt Travelling Scholarship, 1923, and Honan Scholarship, 1924. Dip.Arch. 1925. Awarded Henry Jarvis Studentship, tenable at the British School at Rome, in 1926, having won the competition for the Williamson Art Gallery in partnership with L. G. Hannaford earlier the same year. Other buildings include: Liverpool Orphanage, Woolton Road (in partnership with Barnish and Silcock), 1933–34; Portland Court flats, New Brighton, 1938; Nautical Catering College, Canning Place, Liverpool, 1965–66. Taught at Liverpool School of Architecture from 1930.

Refs: Obituary, *JRIBA*, July 1971, p. 310; British School at Rome, Jarvis Scholar file; family papers; student record card.

TOWNSEND, Arthur Cecil 1896–1993

Attended Borslem College, Eastbourne, and Liverpool School of Art. Entered Liverpool School of Architecture on an ex-service grant, 1919; Dip.Arch. and Cert.Civic Design, 1923. Practised in Liverpool in partnership with Chalmers Hutton until obtaining a teaching post at Southsea School of Art, Portsmouth, 1929. Became head of Portsmouth School of Architecture.

Refs: student record card.

VELARDE, Francis Xavier 1897–1960

Of Spanish descent on his father's side. Entered Liverpool School of Architecture 1920. Awarded Honan travelling scholarship 1923. Dip.Arch. 1924. Practised chiefly as a church architect, working mainly on Merseyside and in the North West of England. Works include: St Matthew, Clubmoor, Liverpool, 1927; St Gabriel, Blackburn, 1932–33; Our Lady of Lourdes School, Birkdale, Southport, 1935–36; St Monica, Bootle, 1936; Holy Cross, Bidston, Birkenhead, 1959. RIBA Godwin and Wimperis Bursary, 1937. Taught at Liverpool School of Architecture for many years from 1928.

Refs: obituaries, *JRIBA*, May 1961, p. 264 (by Herbert Thearle, q.v.) and *Guardian*, 12 January 1961 (by William Holford, q.v.); student record card.

WELSH, Stephen 1892–1976

Born in Forfar, served articles there. Evening classes at Glasgow School of Architecture. Worked as architectural assistant in Glasgow for two years. Attended Liverpool School of Architecture 1920–22, after war service. 1921 summer vacation with Carrère & Hastings, New York. B.Arch. and Cert.Civic Design, 1922. Rome Scholarship 1922. Worked briefly for Curtis Green 1925–26. 1926–27 held the British School at Rome's first Duveen Scholarship for the study of modern buildings in North America, travelled in USA and Canada and worked for John Russell Pope. Lecturer at Liverpool School of Architecture, 1927–28, in charge of fifth year students. Appointed Head of Department of Architecture at Sheffield University in 1928, Professor in 1948. Buildings include: Students' Union, Sheffield; church of St James and St Christopher, Shiregreen, Sheffield.

Refs: Welsh papers, British Architectural Library, RIBA, manuscripts collection; British School at Rome, Rome Scholar file; student record card.

WILLIAMSON, Frederick

After Manchester School of Technology attended Liverpool School of Architecture between 1913 and 1921. Spent 1920 summer vacation in a New York architect's office. In 1921 joined Frank Emley in Johannesburg to work on the University of the Witwatersrand. Emley & Williamson became a major Johannesburg practice in the 1920s and 1930s, designing renaissance palazzo-style blocks such as Davidson Mansions and Beresford House; the triumphal arch at Hartbeespoortdam; the Witwatersrand Master Builders Association building; and the Anstey's skyscraper. Williamson did the Art Deco-classical Union House, Johannesburg, in collaboration with Stucke & Harrison.

Refs: Clive M. Chipkin, *Johannesburg Style—Architecture and Society 1880s–1960s*, Cape Town, 1993; University Archives, University of Liverpool, photograph album, A152; *Liverpool Post*, 29 October 1920; student record card.

WILLS, Trenwith Lovering 1891–1972

Attended Homewood School, Freshfield, Lancashire. Entered Liverpool School of Architecture 1908; Cert.Arch. 1910. 1910–20 (except for war service) in office of Detmar Blow and Fernand Billerey, working on theatres and houses. Met Gerald Wellesley there. Together they did country house work at Sherfield Court, Hampshire; Inverchapel Lodge, Argyllshire; the Warren House, Stanmore; and Naldridge Manor, Buckinghamshire. They designed premises for Heinemann the publishers at Kingswood, Surrey, and a sitting room for Mrs Payne-Thompson at 20 Belgrave Square, London. Wills did war memorials at the Royal School of Mines, the RIBA and the Royal Academy, as well as at Hightown north of Liverpool, all in collaboration with Herbert Tyson Smith. He became a member of the Architecture Club in 1922.

Refs: obituary, *Building*, 13 October 1972, p. 100; student record card.

WRIGHT, Lawrence 1906–1983

Attended Merchant Taylors School, Crosby. Entered Liverpool School of Architecture 1924. As a student designed decorations for Castle Street during 1927 Royal visit to Liverpool. B. Arch. 1929. Designed mural decorations for Century Theatre, Liverpool. Owen Jones Studentship, RIBA, 1932. MA 1934. After graduation made a career as a perspectivist, showing as many as nineteen drawings of other architects' work in one RA Summer Exhibition. Panoramas of London by Wright are in the Museum of London. In 1930s and 1940s made animated films including, under pseudonym Lance White, a satire about Hitler called *Adolf's Busy Day*. Publications include *Perspective in Perspective*, 1983.

Refs: Page L. Dickinson, 'Lawrence Wright and his Work', *Pencil Points*, May 1931, pp. 327–42; British Architectural Library, RIBA, biography file; student record card.